Andy.

Capital gains tax (p. 80)

Exemptions and reliefs	200[illegible]		
Annual exempt amount	7,200	7,100	6,800
Chattel exemption (max. sale proceeds)	6,000	6,000	6,000
Maximum retirement relief	375,000	500,000	625,000

Inheritance tax (p. 93)

	Gross rate of tax	
	Transfers on death	Lifetime transfers
Gross cumulative transfer (on or after 6 April 2000) £	%	%
1–234,000	Nil	Nil
234,001 upwards	40	20

Note
Estate on death taxed as top slice of cumulative transfers in the seven years before death. Most lifetime transfers (other than to discretionary trusts) are potentially exempt, only becoming chargeable where death occurs within seven years.

Annual exemption	£3,000
Small gift exemption	£250

VAT (p. 106)

Standard rate	17.5%
Annual registration limit – taxable supplies (from 1 April 2000)	£52,000
De-registration limit – taxable supplies (from 1 April 2000)	£50,000
VAT fraction	7/47

Insurance premium tax (p. 118)

	Standard rate	Higher rate
From 1 July 1999	5%	17.5%
From 1 April 1997 to 30 June 1999	4%	17.5%

Landfill tax (p. 119)

Period	Standard rate per tonne £	Higher rate per tonne £
1 April 2004–31 March 2005	2	15
1 April 2003–31 March 2004	2	14
1 April 2002–31 March 2003	2	13
1 April 2001–31 March 2002	2	12
April 2000–31 March 2001	2	11
1 April 1999–31 March 2000	2	10
1 October 1996–31 March 1999	2	7

01236 736121

National Insurance contributions (p. 39)

Class 1 primary (employee) contributions 2000–2001	
Lower earnings limit (LEL)	£67 weekly
Primary threshold	£76 weekly
Rate on earnings up to primary threshold	0%
Not contracted-out rate on earnings between primary threshold and upper earnings limit (UEL)	10%
Contracted-out rate on earnings between primary threshold and upper earnings limit (UEL)	8.4%
Reduced rate on earnings between primary threshold and UEL	3.85%
Upper earnings limit	£535 weekly

Class 1 secondary (employer) contributions 2000–2001	
Earnings threshold	£84 weekly
Not contracted-out rate	12.2% above earnings threshold
Contracted-out rates	9.2% for salary-related (COSR) and 11.6% for money-purchase (COMP) schemes (including 3% and 0.6% rebates for earnings from LEL to earnings threshold), then 12.2% above UEL.

Class 2 – Self-employed	**2000–2001**	**1999–2000**	**1998–99**
	£	£	£
Small earnings exemption limit (annual)	3,825	3,770	3,590
Weekly rate	2.00	6.55	6.35

Class 3 – Voluntary contributions	**2000–2001**	**1999–2000**	**1998–99**
	£	£	£
Weekly rate	6.55	6.45	6.25

Class 4 – Self-employed	**2000–2001**	**1999–2000**	**1998–99**
	£	£	£
Annual earnings limit – upper	27,820	26,000	25,220
– lower	4,385	7,530	7,310
Maximum contributions	1,640.45	1,108.20	1,074.60
Rate	7%	6%	6%

Preface

Now in its 16th edition *Hardman's Tax Rates & Tables* contains the numerical and factual data in everyday use by the tax practitioner. The material is conveniently arranged in ten sections: income tax, National Insurance contributions, corporation tax, general, capital gains tax, inheritance tax, stamp duties, value added tax, insurance premium tax and landfill tax.

The booklet contains the latest available data at the time of going to press. It takes full account of the measures contained in the Finance Bill 2000, which was published on 7 April 2000 and of other changes announced by the Chancellor of the Exchequer in his March 2000 Budget speech. The data may be affected by amendments made to the Bill during its passage through Parliament. Foreign exchange rates to December 1999 and March 2000 are published later in the year. These, together with any other information, for example *Finance Act* 2000 changes, will be issued in a free supplement later in the year.

Every effort has been taken to include, within the constraints of available space, the information of greatest use to the practitioner. A number of changes have been made in the light of suggestions received from users of previous years' editions. Croner.CCH welcomes further suggestions as to material which might be inserted in future editions.

24 May 2000

Note: The late Philip Hardman was the original editor of this publication and Croner.CCH remains grateful for his considerable help and guidance.

Important disclaimer

This publication is intended to provide accurate information in regard to the subject matter covered. Readers entering into transactions on the basis of such information should seek the services of a competent professional adviser as this publication is sold on the understanding that the publisher is not engaged in rendering legal or accounting advice or other professional services. The publisher and the editors expressly disclaim all and any liability and responsibility to any person, whether a purchaser or reader of this publication or not, in respect of anything and of the consequences of anything, done or omitted to be done by any such person in reliance, whether wholly or partially, upon the whole or any part of the contents of this publication.

The publisher advises that any materials issued by other bodies and reproduced in this publication are not the authorised official versions of those materials. In their preparation, however, the greatest care has been taken to ensure exact conformity with the material as issued. While copyright in that material resides in the relevant body, copyright in the remaining material in this publication is vested in the publisher.

Ownership of Trade Mark

The trade mark CRONER CCH is the property of

Croner.CCH Group Ltd

ISBN 0 86325 550-7
ISSN 1467-3258

Croner.CCH Group Ltd
Telford Road, Bicester, Oxfordshire OX6 0XD
Telephone +44(0)1869 253300, Facsimile +44(0)1869 874700

Typeset and printed in the UK by Croner.CCH Group Ltd.
Bound in the UK by Information Press, Eynsham, Oxfordshire.

About the Publisher

Croner.CCH is part of the Wolters Kluwer Group. Wolters Kluwer is the leading international publisher specialising in tax, business and law publishing throughout Europe, the US and the Asia Pacific region. The group produces a wide range of information services in different media for the accounting and legal professions and for business. The UK operation also acts as distributor of the publications of the overseas affiliates.

All Croner.CCH publications are designed to be practical and authoritative reference works and guides and are written by our own highly qualified and experienced editorial team and specialist outside authors.

Croner.CCH publishes information packages including electronic products, loose-leaf reporting services, newsletters and books on UK and European legal topics for distribution world-wide. The UK operation also acts as distributor of the publications of the overseas affiliates.

Croner.CCH
Telford Road
Bicester
Oxfordshire
OX6 0XD
Telephone: (01869) 253300

Croner.CCH Group Ltd,
Croner House, London Road, Kingston-upon-Thames,
Surrey, KT2 6SR. Part of the Wolters Kluwer Group
Telephone: 020 8547 3333

Acknowledgements

Certain material in this publication is Crown copyright and is reproduced with the kind permission of the Controller of Her Majesty's Stationery Office.

Croner.CCH kindly acknowledges the endorsement of this publication by the Chartered Institute of Taxation and the Tax Faculty of the Institute of Chartered Accountants in England and Wales.

THE CHARTERED INSTITUTE OF TAXATION

THE INSTITUTE OF CHARTERED ACCOUNTANTS IN ENGLAND & WALES

INCOME TAX

Personal allowances and reliefs 1995–96 to 2000–2001

Type of relief	2000–2001 £	1999–2000 £	1998–99 £	1997–98 £	1996–97 £	1995–96 £
Personal allowance						
Age under 65	4,385	4,335	4,195	4,045	3,765	3,525
Age 65–74[4]	5,790	5,720	5,410	5,220	4,910	4,630
Age 75 & over[4]	6,050	5,980	5,600	5,400	5,090	4,800
Married couple's allowance[1][2][3]						
Age under 65	–	1,970	1,900	1,830	1,790	1,720
Age 65–74[4]	5,185	5,125	3,305	3,185	3,115	2,995
Age 75 & over[4]	5,255	5,195	3,345	3,225	3,155	3,035
Monthly reduction in year of marriage:						
Age under 65	–	164.16	158.33	152.50	149.17	143.33
Age 65–74 pre 6 April 2000	432.08	427.08	275.42	265.42	259.58	249.58
Age 75 & over	437.92	432.91	278.75	268.75	262.92	252.92
Maximum income before abatement of relief for taxpayers aged 65 and over	17,000	16,800	16,200	15,600	15,200	14,600
Abatement income ceiling[5]						
Personal						
– Age 65–74	19,810	19,570	18,630	17,950	17,490	16,810
– Age 75 & over	20,330	20,090	19,010	18,310	17,850	17,150
Married						
– Age 65–74	26,180	25,880	21,440	20,660	20,140	19,360
– Age 75 & over	26,840	26,540	21,900	21,100	20,580	19,780
Additional allowance for children[1][2]	–	1,970	1,900	1,830	1,790	1,720
Widow's bereavement allowance[1][2]	2,000[1]	1,970	1,900	1,830	1,790	1,720
Blind person's allowance	1,400	1,380	1,330	1,280	1,250	1,200
Life assurance relief (policies issued before 14 March 1984)[6]	12.5% of premiums	12.5% of premiums	12.5% of premiums	12.5% of premiums	12.5% of premiums	12.5% of premiums
Mortgage interest: Loan limit[7]	–	30,000	30,000	30,000	30,000	30,000
'Rent-a-room' Limit[8]	4,250	4,250	4,250	4,250	3,250	3,250

Notes

[1] From 6 April 2000 the married couple's allowance, additional personal allowance and relief for maintenance payments are withdrawn, and widow's bereavement allowance is withdrawn for new claimants. The children's tax credit will be introduced from April 2001, and replaces the married couple's allowance.

[2] For 1999–2000 relief for married couple's allowance, and other reliefs linked to it, is restricted to 10% (1995–96 to 1998–99 15%; 1994–95 20%).

[3] From 6 April 1993 the MCA may, irrespective of the husband's level of income, be allocated to the wife or split equally between them.

[4] After 5 April 1990 a claimant is entitled to the appropriate age personal allowance if he/she is 65/75 or over at any time in the tax year; the allowance is restricted according to his/her income only. After 5 April 1990 married couples are entitled to the appropriate age married couple's allowance if either spouse is 65/75 or over at any time in the tax year; the allowance is restricted only according to the income of the husband.

[5] From 6 April 1989 relief is abated by $^1/_2$ total income over the maximum income limit (previously $^2/_3$ total income over the maximum income limit) subject to the abatement income ceiling. The age-related married couples allowance cannot be reduced below £2,000 for 2000–2001.

[6] Life assurance relief withdrawn for most policies issued after 13 March 1984.

(7) Mortgage interest relief on loans for home purchase is withdrawn from 6 April 2000. From the same date relief is also withdrawn for loans made prior to 6 April 1988 for home improvements or the purchase or improvement of homes for a dependent relative (or for the borrower's divorced or separated spouse).
(8) Gross annual rents from furnished letting of rooms in only or main residence exempt for owner occupiers up to specified limit (F(No. 2)A 1992, s. 59 and Sch. 10): If more than one person is in receipt of income from furnished residential accommodation in the residence, the exempt limit is halved.

Tax credits

Working families tax credit (WFTC)[1][2]

Credits payable from October 1999 onwards

		2000–2001	1999–2000
Basic tax credit		£53.15	£52.30
Credit where one earner works at least 30 hours per week		£11.25	£11.05
Child tax credits	Under 11	£21.25	£19.85
	11–16	£21.25	£20.90
	16–18	£26.35	£25.95
Childcare tax credit		70% of eligible childcare costs up to a maximum of: • £100 a week costs for one child (i.e. maximum of £70 credit); and • £150 a week for more than one (i.e. maximum of £105 credit).	70% of eligible childcare costs up to a maximum of: • £100 a week costs for one child (i.e. maximum of £70 credit); and • £150 a week for more than one (i.e. maximum of £105 credit).
Tapered clawback where net income over weekly threshold		• 55p for each £1 of net income in excess of £91.45 per week.	• 55p for each £1 of net income in excess of £90.00 per week.

Notes
(1) The withdrawal rate is at 55% of every pound of net family income over the threshold of £91.45 per week for 2000–2001 (£90 per week for 1999–2000). Savings limit is £8,000.
(2) The WFTC replaces family credit. WFTC is administered by the Revenue and paid through wage packets from April 2000. Self-employed people receive WFTC direct from the Revenue. Couples are able to choose whether the mother or father receives the WFTC. WFTC award is calculated by adding the credits together. WFTC award will normally last for 26 weeks.

Disabled person's tax credit (DPTC)[1][2]

		2000–2001	1999–2000
Basic tax credit	Single person	£55.15	£54.30
	Couple or lone parent	£84.90	£83.55
Credit where claimant or partner works at least 30 hours per week		£11.25	£11.05
Child tax credits	Under 11	£21.25	£19.85
	11–16	£21.25	£20.90
	16–18	£26.35	£25.95
	Disabled child	£22.25	£21.90
Childcare tax credit		70% of eligible childcare costs up to a maximum of: • £100 a week costs for one child (i.e. maximum of £70 credit); and • £150 a week for more than one (i.e. maximum of £105 credit).	70% of eligible childcare costs up to a maximum of: • £100 a week costs for one child (i.e. maximum of £70 credit); and • £150 a week for more than one (i.e. maximum of £105 credit).
Tapered clawback where net income over weekly threshold		• 55p for each £1 of net income in excess of £71.10 a week (single person) or £91.45 a week (couple or lone parent).	• 55p for each £1 of net income in excess of £70.00 a week (single person) or £90.00 a week (couple or lone parent).

Notes

(1) The claimant must not have more than £16,000 savings.

(2) The DPTC replaces disability working allowance. It is payable to a claimant with an illness or disability which puts them at a disadvantage in getting a job and who has one of a number of qualifying benefits. It is administered by the Inland Revenue and paid through wage packets from April 2000.

Income tax rates 1994–95 to 2000–2001

	2000–2001 Taxable income £	**Tax £**	**1999–2000 Taxable income £**	**Tax £**	**1998–99 Taxable income £**	**Tax £**
Lower rate	1,520 @ 10% =	152	1,500 @ 10% =	150	4,300 @ 20% =	860
Basic rate[1]	1,521–28,400 @ 22% =	5,913	1,501–28,000 @ 23% =	6,095	4,301–27,100 @ 23% =	5,244
		6,065		6,245		6,104
Higher rate	over 28,400 @ 40%		over 28,000 @ 40%		over 27,100 @ 40%	
Additional rate (accumulation and discretionary trusts)	flat rate of 34% applicable to trusts		flat rate of 34% applicable to trusts		flat rate of 34% applicable to trusts	

	1997–98 Taxable income £	**Tax £**	**1996–97 Taxable income £**	**Tax £**	**1995–96 Taxable income £**	**Tax £**
Lower rate	4,100 @ 20% =	820	3,900 @ 20% =	780	3,200 @ 20% =	640
Basic rate	4,101–26,100 @ 23% =	5,060	3,901–25,500 @ 24% =	5,184	3,201–24,300 @ 25% =	5,275
		5,880		5,964		5,915
Higher rate	over 26,100 @ 40%		over 25,500 @ 40%		over 24,300 @ 40%	
Additional rate (accumulation and discretionary trusts)	10% (rate applicable to trusts 34%)		10% (rate applicable to trusts 35%)		10% (rate applicable to trusts 35%)	

	1994–95 Taxable income £	**Tax £**
Lower rate	3,000 @ 20% =	600
Basic rate	3,001–23,700 @ 25% =	5,175
		5,775
Higher rate	over 23,700 @ 40%	
Additional rate (accumulation and discretionary trusts)	10% (rate applicable to trusts 35%)	

Note

[1] For 2000–2001, savings income, other than dividends, is generally taxed at 20% for income below the basic rate limit and at 40% above that. UK dividend income is taxed at 10% up to the basic rate limit and at 32.5% thereafter.

Submission of personal tax returns

The return for 2000–2001 must be filed by 31 January 2002, except in the following circumstances:

Circumstances	Filing date
Taxpayer wishes the inspector to calculate the tax liability or repayment:	
• return issued by 31 July 2001	30 September 2001
• return issued after 31 July 2001	Two months from date of issue
Taxpayer making self-assessment – return issued after 31 October 2001	Three months from date of issue
Taxpayer wishes underpayment (below £1,000) to be coded out under 2001–2002 PAYE	30 September 2001

Main penalty provisions: individuals

Offence	Penalty[1][2]
Late return (TMA 1970, s. 93)[3][4]:	
• short delay	£100
• delay of six months or more	£100
• delay of 12 months or more	Tax geared
• on application to the commissioners	Up to £60 per day
Failure to notify chargeability	Tax geared (TMA 1970, s. 7)
Incorrect return, accounts and claims	Tax geared (TMA 1970, s. 95)
Failure to keep and retain tax records	Up to £3,000 per year of assessment (TMA 1970, s. 12B)
False statements to reduce interim payments	Tax geared (TMA 1970, s. 59A)
Failure to produce documents in an investigation:	
• initial penalty	£50
• daily penalty	£30/£150[5]

Notes

(1) Interest is charged on penalties not paid when due. The due date is 30 days after the notice of determination of the penalty is issued.

(2) A defence of 'reasonable excuse' may be available.

(3) Late return penalties are cumulative, e.g. for a return six or more months late there are two £100 penalties.

(4) The two fixed £100 penalties are reduced if the total tax payable by assessment is less than the penalty which would otherwise be chargeable.

(5) The lower daily rate applies when determination of the penalty was made by the inspector, the higher when determination was made by the commissioners.

Main penalty provisions: partnerships

Offence	Penalty[1][2]
Late return (TMA 1970, s. 93A)[3][4]:	
• short delay	£100
• delay of six months or more	£100
• on application to the commissioners	Up to £60 per day
Failure to notify chargeability	None
Incorrect return, accounts and claims	Tax geared (TMA 1970, s. 95A)
Failure to keep and retain tax records	Up to £3,000 per year of assessment (TMA 1970, s. 12B)
Failure to produce documents in an investigation:	
• initial penalty	£50
• daily penalty	£30/£150[5]

Notes

[1] Interest is charged on penalties not paid when due. The due date is 30 days after the notice of determination of the penalty is issued.

[2] A defence of 'reasonable excuse' on the part of the representative partner or his successor may be available.

[3] Late return penalties are cumulative, e.g. for a return six or more months late there are two £100 penalties.

[4] Late return penalties apply to each partner (e.g. short delay = £100 per partner).

[5] The lower daily rate applies when determination of the penalty was made by the inspector, the higher when determination was made by the commissioners.

PAYE thresholds

(Income Tax (Employments) Regulations 1993 (SI 1993/744), reg. 28(2))

Period	Pay days	Amount	
		Weekly £	Monthly £
2000–2001	6 April 2000	84.00	365.00
1999–2000	6 April 1999 to 5 April 2000	83.00	359.60
1998–99	6 April 1998 to 5 April 1999	80.50	349.50
1997–98	6 April 1997 to 5 April 1998	78.00	337.00
1996–97	6 April 1996 to 5 April 1997	72.50	314.00
1995–96	6 April 1995 to 5 April 1996	68.00	294.00
1994–95	6 April 1993 to 5 April 1995	66.50	287.00

Note
Under normal circumstances, employers need not deduct tax for employees who earn less than the above amounts.

PAYE code numbers

The PAYE code enables an employer or payer of pension to make any changes announced in the budget. The codes are as follows:

L for a code with basic personal allowance.
A liable at higher rate of tax for a code with basic personal allowance plus the basic married couple's allowance or additional personal allowance.
H liable at basic rate of tax for a code with basic personal allowance plus the basic married couple's allowance or additional personal allowance.
J liable at lower rate of tax for a code with basic personal allowance plus the basic married couple's allowance or additional personal allowance.
P for a code with personal allowance for those aged 65–74.
V for a code with the personal allowance for those aged 65–74 plus the married couple's allowance for those aged 65–74.
T in most other cases where L, H, P or V does not apply or where the employee:

- asks the Revenue not to use L, H, P or V; or
- gets the increased age allowance for those aged 75/80 and over; or
- does not get the full age allowance because his income is more than the maximum income limit; or
- has a deduction for a car benefit in his code.

However, there are five special codes which do not have numbers or which have numbers which do not show the amount of the allowances.

BR means that no allowances have been given. Tax will be deducted at basic rate.
D (followed by a number) means that tax is to be deducted at a higher rate.
K (followed by a number) means that the person's benefits and other adjustments are more than his allowances.
NT means that no tax is to be deducted.
OT means that no allowances have been given. Tax will be deducted at basic rate, then at the higher rate depending on the income.

If the code contains the letters T or K and the allowances change in the Budget, the Revenue will work out the new code and tell the employee and his employer what it is, usually on form P2.

PAYE returns

Deadlines

Forms	Date	Provision	Penalty provisions
P14, P35, P38 and P38A[1]	19 May following tax year	*Income Tax (Employment) Regulations* 1993 (SI 1993/744), reg. 43	TMA 1970, s. 98A
P60 (to employee) (1996/97 and later years)	31 May following tax year	*Income Tax (Employments) Regulations* 1993, reg. 39 as amended by *Income Tax (Employments) (Amendment No. 4) Regulations* 1995	TMA 1970, s. 98A
P9D and P11D (1996/97 and later years)	6 July following tax year	*Income Tax (Employments) Regulations* 1993, reg. 46 as amended by *Income Tax (Employments) (Amendment No. 4) Regulations* 1995	TMA 1970, s. 98
P46 (Car) (1994/95 and later years)	3 May, 2 August, 2 November, 2 February	*Income Tax (Employments) Regulations* 1993, reg. 46A	TMA 1970, s. 98

Notes

[1] For 1994–95 onwards, penalties are levied on late returns automatically.

Penalties that may be imposed for delays

Forms	Initial	Continuing	Delay exceeds 12 months
P14, P35, P38 and P38A[2]	Up to £1,200[1] per 50 employees	£100 monthly per 50 employees	Penalty not exceeding 100%[1] of the tax or NICs payable for the year of assessment but not paid by 19 April following the end of the year of assessment
Forms P9D and P11D	£300 per return[1]	£60 per day[1]	

Notes

[1] This penalty is mitigable.

[2] From 20 May 1995 an automatic non-mitigable penalty applies as follows:

up to 12 months	£100 per 50 employees chargeable for each month return delayed
end 12 months	monthly penalty ceases to accrue additional penalty (not fixed) to be charged

Penalties that may be imposed for incorrect returns

Forms	Provision TMA 1970	Penalty
P14, P35, P38 and P38A	s. 98A	Maximum of 100% of tax underpaid (s. 98A(4))
P9D and P11D	s. 98	Maximum penalty £3,000 (s. 98(2))

Interest on PAYE paid late

Interest on certain late payments of PAYE was introduced from 19 April 1993 in relation to 1992–93 and subsequent tax years (*Income Tax (Employments) Regulations* 1993 (SI 1993/744), reg. 51).

Where an employer has not paid the net tax deductible by him to the collector within 14 days of the end of the tax year, the unpaid tax carries interest at the prescribed rate from the reckonable date until the date of payment. Certain repayments of tax also attract interest.

Income tax normal due dates: 2000–2001

For 1997–98 onwards tax is paid on 31 January following the year of assessment as a single sum covering capital gains tax and income tax on all sources. Interim payments on account (income tax only) may be required[(1)]. These will normally be half the amount of the net tax payable for the preceding year, but may be reduced to half the current year's liability if less. For 2000–2001 the following due dates apply:

First interim payment	31 January 2001
Second interim payment	31 July 2001
Final balancing payment	31 January 2002

Notes

[(1)] No interim payments are required for a year of assessment if the tax paid by assessment for the preceding year was less than £500 or 20% of the total tax liability for that year.

Farming and market gardening: relief for fluctuating profits

(ICTA 1988, s. 96)

Full averaging (ICTA 1988, s. 96(2))

Applies where profits for either relevant tax year do not exceed 70 per cent of profits for the other year or are nil.

Marginal averaging (ICTA 1988, s. 96(3))

Computation of adjustment to the profits of each relevant tax year:

3((75% H) − L) where:

H is the higher profit; and
L is the lower profit.

Personal pension contributions (PPCs) and retirement annuity premiums (RAPs)

Tax year	Age of taxpayer at the *beginning* of the tax year (ICTA 1988, s. 626, 640(2))	Limit of allowable payment	
		PPCs %	RAPs %
1993–94 to 2000–2001	35 or less	17.5	17.5
	36–45	20	17.5
	46–50	25	17.5
	51–55	30	20
	56–60	35	22.5
	61–75	40	27.5

Carry-forward of relief: in calculating the maximum relief deductible in a year the relief (not premiums/contributions paid) which was not used in an earlier year can be carried forward and used in any of the following six years (ICTA 1988, s. 625, 642). Relief which is carried forward is used on a first-in, first-out basis.

Carry-back of contributions or premiums: an individual can elect to treat all or part of a payment made in one year as if it was paid in the last preceding year, or if he had *no* 'net relevant earnings' in that last preceding year then he can elect to treat it as paid in the last preceding year but one (ICTA 1988, s. 619(4), 641(1); Form 43, PP42 and PP43 in respect of retirement annuity premiums and personal pension contributions respectively).

Where an individual pays both PPCs and RAPs maximum allowable PPCs (computed by reference to the earnings cap or otherwise) are reduced by qualifying RAPs paid and given relief in the tax year (ICTA 1988, s. 655(1)).

Personal pension contributions (PPCs) earnings cap

(ICTA 1988, s. 640A, 646A)

Tax year	Maximum pensionable earnings £
2000–2001	91,800
1999–2000	90,600
1998–99	87,600
1997–98	84,000
1996–97	82,200
1995–96	78,600
1994–95	76,800

Note

The earnings cap also applies for various purposes relating to occupational pension schemes (ICTA 1988, s. 590B, 590C, 592, 594, 599).

Partners

(ICTA 1988, s. 628)

The earned income limit for a retirement annuity paid to a former partner is 50 per cent of the average of his share of the partnership profits in the best three of the last seven years in which he was a partner.

The former partner's share of the profits in the first six of the last seven years in which he was a partner is increased by the percentage increase in the RPI from the December in the relevant year to the December in the seventh year. The RPI is reproduced on p. 82.

Early retirement ages: retirement annuity contracts and personal pension schemes

The early retirement ages shown in the table on p. 13 have been agreed by the Revenue under ICTA 1988, s. 620(4)(c) (approval of retirement annuity contracts) and under the provisions of ICTA 1988, s. 634(3)(b) for personal pension schemes. Individuals in other professions or occupations may not normally take benefits from their pension arrangements before age 60 in the case of retirement annuity contracts and before 50 in the case of personal pension schemes except in the case of retirement owing to illness or disability. For personal pension schemes see also Revenue Booklet IR 76.

Profession or occupation	Retirement age	
	Retirement annuity contracts	Personal pension schemes
Air pilots	55	–
Athletes (appearance and prize money)	35	35
Badminton players	35	35
Boxers	35	35
Brass instrumentalists	55	–
Cricketers	40	40
Croupiers	50	–
Cyclists	35	35
Dancers	35	35
Divers (saturation, deep sea and free swimming)	40	40
Firemen (part-time)	55	–
Fishermen (inshore or distant water trawlermen)	55	–
Footballers	35	35
Golfers (tournament earnings)	40	40
Interdealer brokers	50	–
Jockeys – flat racing	45	45
– National Hunt	35	35
Martial arts instructors	50	–
Models	35	35
Moneybroker dealers	50	–
Moneybroker dealer directors and managers responsible for dealers	55	–
Motorcycle riders (motocross or road racing)	40	40
Motor racing drivers	40	40
Newscasters (ITV)	50	–
Nurses, physiotherapists, midwives or health visitors who are females	55	–
Off-shore riggers	50	–
Psychiatrists (who are also maximum part-time specialists employed within the National Health Services solely in the treatment of the mentally disordered)	55	–
Royal Naval reservists	50	–
Royal Marine reservists non-commissioned	45	45
Rugby League players	35	35
Rugby League referees	50	–
Skiers (downhill)	–	30
Singers	55	–
Speedway riders	40	40
Squash players	35	35
Table tennis players	35	35
Tennis players (including real tennis)	35	35
Territorial Army members	50	–
Trapeze artistes	40	40
Wrestlers	35	35

Notes
The pension age shown applies only to pension arrangements funded by contributions paid in respect of the relevant earnings from the occupation or profession carrying that age. If an individual wishes to make pension provisions in respect of another source of relevant earnings to which the pension age shown above does not apply then a separate arrangement, with a pension age within the normal range, must be made.
In particular, the ages shown above for professional sportsmen apply only to arrangements made in respect of relevant earnings from activities as professional sportsmen, e.g. tournament earnings, appearance and prize money. They do not apply to relevant earnings from sponsorship or coaching.

Payments on loss of office and employment

(ICTA 1988, Sch. 11)

Period	Relief
1993–94 to 2000–2001	£30,000 exempt

Notes

The Revenue will not charge tax on legal costs incurred by a former employee or office holder in a court action to recover compensation for loss of employment, where those costs were recovered under a court order or, under certain circumstances, an out-of-court settlement (ESC A81). The concession does not apply to other professional costs.

In relation to ex gratia payments, see SP 13/91, SFO Memoranda No. 104 and 111, ICAEW Technical Release TR 851 and Law Society's *Gazette*, 7 October 1992. (The SFO is now known as the Pensions Schemes Office.)

All-employee share plan

	Free Shares	Partnership Shares	Matching Shares	Dividend Shares
Employment before eligibility(1)	Up to 12 months employment	Up to 12 months employment	Only awarded to employees who buy partnership shares	Must be acquired with dividends from plan shares
Limits	Up to £3,000 per tax year	Up to £1,500 per tax year, capped at lower of: £125 per month and 10% of monthly salary	Up to 2 matching shares for each partnership share bought	Dividends from shares in the plan reinvested: — £500 in 1st year — £1,000 in 2nd year — £1,500 per year thereafter
Minimum amount if stated(1)	—	£10 per month	—	
Performance measures(1)	Yes	No	No	No
Holding period	At least 3 years from award(2)	None	At least 3 years from award(2)	3 years from acquisition
Forfeiture on cessation of employment(1)	Yes	No	Yes	No
Tax on award	None	None – tax relief for salary used to buy shares	None	None
Tax on removal of shares from plan within 3 years of award(3)	On market value when taken out	On market value when taken out	On market value when taken out	Original dividend taxable but in year when shares taken out of plan.
Tax on removal between 3 and 5 years of award(2)	On lower of: – value at award; & – value on removal	On lower of: – salary used to buy shares; & – value on removal	On lower of: – value at award; & – value on removal	None
Tax on removal after 5 years	None	None	None	None
CGT on removal – any time	None	None	None	None

Notes

(1) These conditions can be included at the option of the company

(2) The holding period may be up to 5 years at the option of the company

(3) PAYE and NICs will be operated in relation to any Schedule E income tax charge where the shares are readily convertible assets.

Approved profit sharing schemes

(ICTA 1988, s. 186, 187 and Sch. 9, 10)

Maximum value of shares	
From 6/4/91	Greater of £3,000 or 10% of salary, up to £8,000

Notes

- No further tax-free awards can be made under the APS from April 2002.

With effect from 29 April 1996, the *Finance Act* 1996 reduced the period for which shares must be held in trust from five to three years. For income tax payable on early sale the appropriate percentage is now:

- 100% before the third anniversary;
- 0% on or after third anniversary;
- 50% if the taxpayer ceases to be a director or employee of the grantor (or participating company), or reaches an age between 60 and 75.

The appropriate percentage for excess or unauthorised shares is 100% in every case.

Company share option plans

(ICTA 1988, s. 185, 187 and Sch. 9)

From 26 April 1996 the maximum value of shares under option which can be held by an employee at any one time is £30,000.

In respect of options granted on or after 29 July 1996, the price at which the option may be exercised must not be manifestly less than market value at the time the option is granted or an earlier time agreed by the Revenue in writing and provided in the agreement.

Approved savings-related share option schemes

(ICTA 1988, s. 185, 187 and Sch. 9)

Monthly contributions

Period	Maximum	Minimum
From 1/4/96	£250	£5 to £10[1]
From 1/9/91 to 31/3/96	£250	£10

Notes

[1] The company may choose a minimum savings contribution of between £5 and £10.

The maximum permissible discount on shares acquired under a scheme is 20% of the market value at the time of the grant of options.

Bonus and interest payments on termination

Date of termination	Amount payable
3-year contract	
After at least 1 but less than 3 years	Refund of contributions plus interest at 3%
After 3 years	Refund of contributions plus bonus of 3 months' contributions
5-year contract	
After at least 1 but less than 5 years	Refund of contributions plus interest at 3%
After 5 years	Refund of contributions plus bonus of 9 months' contributions
After at least 5 but less than 7 years	Refund of contributions plus bonus of 9 months' contributions and interest at 3% for period after first 5 years
After 7 years	Refund of contributions plus bonus of 18 months' contributions

Enterprise Management Incentives (EMI)

Qualifying Company	Gross assets not exceeding £15m
Qualifying employees	Up to 15
Maximum options	Up to £100,000 per employee

Profit-related pay schemes

(ICTA 1988, s. 169ff. and Sch. 8)

Profit periods	Limit on tax-free amount
Beginning on or after 1 January 2000	No relief available
Beginning on or after 1 January 1999	Lower of 20% of earnings and £1,000
Beginning on or after 1 January 1998	Lower of 20% of earnings and £2,000
Beginning on or after 1 April 1991	Lower of 20% of earnings and £4,000

Car benefit scales 1993–94 to 2000–2001

Car benefit scales 1999–2000 to 2000–2001

	Percentage of manufacturer's list price (maximum £80,000 price)	
	Number of cars available concurrently to employee	
Age of car at end of tax year under 4 years	First car %	Second and subsequent cars %
Business miles		
Less than 2,500 miles	35	35
2,500 miles to 17,999 miles	25	35
18,000 miles or more	15	25
Age of car at end of tax year 4 years or more The percentages above are reduced by $^1/_4$.		

Notes

The cash equivalent benefit and the business mileage limits are reduced proportionately where a car is 'unavailable' for 30 or more consecutive days, or where an employee starts or ceases to have use of the car part way through the year (ICTA 1988, Sch. 6, para. 3, 6 and 9).

The car benefit charge is reduced by any amount which the employee is required to pay as a condition of the car being available for his private use. If the amount exceeds the cash equivalent, the charge is reduced to nil (ICTA 1988, Sch. 6, para. 7).

Generally, the manufacturer's list price is the price of the car published by the manufacturer, distributor or importer of the car when the car was registered, including VAT and any other relevant tax and delivery charge together with the published price for optional accessories (excluding any mobile phone) provided with the car either when first provided or at a later date (subject to a £100 de minimis limit) (ICTA 1988, s. 168A). Where the manufacturer's price list is not available, the Revenue will accept prices taken from published guides (Revenue press release, 27 September 1993). Where an employee contributes towards the capital cost of the car or to qualifying accessories the price is permanently reduced by all capital sums contributed by the employee, subject to an upper limit for the reduction of £5,000 (ICTA 1988, s. 168D(3), (4)). The benefit charge applies to directors and employees earning £8,500 p.a. or over (including benefits) (ICTA 1988, s. 157(1)).

The cost of converting a company car to run on road fuel gases will be ignored in calculating the taxable benefit for 1999–2000 and subsequent years of assessment.

Car benefit scales 1994–95 to 1998–99

Age of car at end of tax year under 4 years	Percentage of manufacturer's list price (maximum £80,000 price)	
	Number of cars available concurrently to employee	
	First car %	Second and subsequent cars %
Business miles		
Less than 2,500 miles	35	35
2,500 miles to 17,999 miles	$23^1/_3$	35
18,000 miles or more	$11^2/_3$	$23^1/_3$
Age of car at end of tax year 4 years or more The percentages above are reduced by $^1/_3$.		

Tax year		Age of car at end of tax year	
		Under 4 years £	4 years or more £
1993–94	**Original market value up to £19,250**		
	1,400cc or less	2,310	1,580
	1,401cc–2,000cc	2,990	2,030
	More than 2,000cc	4,800	3,220
	Up to £19,250; no cylinder capacity		
	Less than £6,000	2,310	1,580
	£6,000 or more but less than £8,500	2,990	2,030
	£8,500 or more but not more than £19,250	4,800	3,220
	Original market value more than £19,250		
	More than £19,250 but not more than £29,000	6,210	4,180
	More than £29,000	10,040	6,660

Car benefit scales 1993–94 to 1998–99

Car benefit scales for 1993–94 to 1998–99 should be read in conjunction with the following notes.

(1) Where business use 2,500 miles or less in relevant year, or additional car(s): increase cash equivalent by 50% (i.e. multiply scale by 1.5) (formerly ICTA 1988, Sch. 6, para. 5).

(2) Where business use 18,000 miles or more in relevant year, reduce cash equivalent by 50% (i.e. divide scale by 2) (formerly ICTA 1988, Sch. 6, para. 3).

(3) The amount of the benefit and the 18,000 and 2,500 mile limits are reduced proportionately if the car was 'unavailable' for 30 or more consecutive days or before or after a particular date (formerly ICTA 1988, Sch. 6, para. 2, 3(2), 5(2) respectively).

(4) The car benefit charge is reduced by any amount which the employee was *required* to pay as a condition of the car being available for his private use. If the amount exceeds the cash equivalent above, the charge is reduced to nil (formerly ICTA 1988, Sch. 6, para. 4).

(5) The car benefit charge applies to directors and employees earning £8,500 p.a. or over (including benefits) (formerly ICTA 1988, s. 157(1)).

National Insurance contributions on cars: see p. 43.

Fuel benefit scales 1994–95 to 2000–2001

Petrol		Cash equivalent £
2000–2001	**Cylinder capacity**	
	1,400cc or less	1,700
	1,401cc–2,000cc	2,170
	More than 2,000cc	3,200
	Original market value; no cylinder capacity	
	Any car	3,200
1999–2000	**Cylinder capacity**	
	1,400cc or less	1,210
	1,401cc–2,000cc	1,540
	More than 2,000cc	2,270
	Original market value; no cylinder capacity	
	Any car	2,270
1998–99	**Cylinder capacity**	
	1,400cc or less	1,010
	1,401cc–2,000cc	1,280
	More than 2,000cc	1,890
	Original market value; no cylinder capacity	
	Any car	1,890
1997–98	**Cylinder capacity**	
	1,400cc or less	800
	1,401cc–2,000cc	1,010
	More than 2,000cc	1,490
	Original market value; no cylinder capacity	
	Any car	1,490
1996–97	**Cylinder capacity**	
	1,400cc or less	710
	1,401cc–2,000cc	890
	More than 2,000cc	1,320
	Original market value; no cylinder capacity	
	Any car	1,320
1995–96	**Cylinder capacity**	
	1,400cc or less	670
	1,401cc–2,000cc	850
	More than 2,000cc	1,260
	Original market value; no cylinder capacity	
	Any car	1,260
1994–95	**Cylinder capacity**	
	1,400cc or less	640
	1,401cc–2,000cc	810
	More than 2,000cc	1,200
	Original market value; no cylinder capacity	
	Any car	1,200

Diesel	Cylinder capacity	Cash equivalent £
2000–2001	2,000cc or less More than 2,000cc	2,170 3,200
1999–2000	2,000cc or less More than 2,000cc	1,540 2,270
1998–99	2,000cc or less More than 2,000cc	1,280 1,890
1997–98	2,000cc or less More than 2,000cc	740 940
1996–97	2,000cc or less More than 2,000cc	640 820
1995–96	2,000cc or less More than 2,000cc	605 780
1994–95	2,000cc or less More than 2,000cc	580 750

Notes

The fuel benefit charge is reduced to nil if the employee is required to make good *all* fuel provided for private use (ICTA 1988, s. 158(6)).

The age of the car is irrelevant for the fuel benefit. The benefit does *not* increase if business use was 2,500 miles or less in the year.

VAT on private fuel: see p. 117.

National Insurance contributions on private fuel: see p. 43.

Van benefit scales

Tax year	Age of van at end of tax year	
	Under 4 years £	4 years or more £
1993–94 to 2000–2001	500	350

Notes

Applies to vehicles weighing 3.5 tonnes or less.

The cash equivalent benefit is reduced proportionately where: the van is unavailable for 30 or more consecutive days; where an employee starts or ceases to have use of the van part way through the year; or where the van is a shared van for part of the year.

The van benefit charge is reduced by any amount which the employee is required to pay as a condition of the van being available for his private use. If the amount exceeds the cash equivalent, the charge is reduced to nil (ICTA 1988, Sch. 6A).

On a claim made by an employee, an alternative calculation may be used. The benefit is calculated as the aggregate of the number of days (including part days) of private use of each van multiplied by £5 (ICTA 1988, Sch. 6A, para. 8(1)–(3)).

The van benefit charge applies to directors and employees earning £8,500 p.a. or over (including benefits) (ICTA 1988, s. 159AA).

Mobile telephones

From 1991–92 to 1998–99 inclusive benefit is £200 a year for each mobile telephone available for private use. No benefit arises where the employee is *required* to, and does, make good the full marginal cost of any private use.

From 6 April 1999 this charge has been abolished.

AA estimated standing and running costs (April 2000 edition)

Petrol cars	Engine capacity (cc)				
	Up to 1,100	1,101 to 1,400	1,401 to 2,000	2,001 to 3,000	3,001 to 4,500
Standing charges per annum (£)					
(a) Road tax	100.00	155.00	155.00	155.00	155.00
(b) Insurance	330.77	440.65	517.51	799.30	825.72
(c) Depreciation (based on 10,000 miles p.a.)	1,117.97	1,646.73	2,328.43	4,208.50	5,776.54
(d) Subscription	75.00	75.00	75.00	75.00	75.00
	1,623.74	2,317.38	3,075.94	5,237.80	6,832.26
Standing charge per mile (pence)					
5,000	32.47	46.35	61.52	104.76	136.65
10,000	16.24	23.17	30.76	52.38	68.32
15,000	12.32	17.64	23.61	40.53	53.25
20,000	11.47	16.53	22.36	38.81	51.49
25,000	10.97	15.86	21.62	37.79	50.44
30,000	9.14	13.21	18.01	31.49	42.03
Running costs per mile (pence)					
(e) Petrol*	9.19	10.51	12.26	16.72	18.39
(f) Oil	0.35	0.36	0.37	0.45	0.71
(g) Tyres	0.76	0.98	1.19	2.29	2.98
(h) Servicing	0.99	0.99	0.99	1.54	2.17
(i) Repairs and replacements	3.11	3.55	3.61	5.52	5.69
pence	14.40	16.39	18.42	26.52	29.94
*Unleaded petrol at 80.9 pence per litre. For every penny more or less add or subtract:	0.11	0.13	0.15	0.21	0.23
Total of standing and running costs (in pence per mile) based on annual mileages of:					
5,000 miles	46.87	62.74	79.94	131.28	166.59
10,000 miles	30.64	39.56	49.18	78.90	98.26
15,000 miles	26.72	34.03	42.03	67.05	83.19
20,000 miles	25.87	32.92	40.78	65.33	81.43
25,000 miles	25.37	32.25	40.04	64.31	80.38
30,000 miles	23.54	29.60	36.43	58.01	71.97

Diesel cars	New purchase price (£)			
	Up to £11,000	£11,001 to £15,000	£15,001 to £20,000	Over £20,001
Standing charges per annum (£)				
(a) Road tax	155.00	155.00	155.00	155.00
(b) Insurance	330.77	440.65	517.51	799.30
(c) Depreciation (based on 10,000 miles p.a.)	1,274.06	1,826.61	2,446.54	3,552.83
(d) Subscription	75.00	75.00	75.00	75.00
	1,834.83	2,497.26	3,194.05	4,582.13
Standing charges per mile (pence)				
5,000	36.70	49.95	63.88	91.64
10,000	18.35	24.97	31.94	45.82
15,000	13.93	19.08	24.56	35.28
20,000	10.45	14.31	18.42	26.46
25,000	9.40	13.37	17.65	25.86
30,000	8.66	11.98	15.54	22.38
Running cost per mile (pence)				
(e) Diesel*	8.27	9.31	9.80	12.41
(f) Oil	0.51	0.51	0.66	0.82
(g) Tyres	0.76	0.98	1.19	2.29
(h) Servicing	1.07	1.07	1.33	1.61
(i) Repairs and replacements	3.11	3.55	3.61	5.52
pence	13.72	15.42	16.59	22.65
* Diesel at 81.9 pence per litre For every penny more or less add or subtract:	0.10	0.11	0.12	0.15
Total of standing and running costs (in pence) based on annual mileages of:				
5,000 miles	50.42	65.37	80.47	114.29
10,000 miles	32.07	40.39	48.53	68.47
15,000 miles	27.65	34.50	41.15	57.93
20,000 miles	24.17	29.73	35.01	49.11
25,000 miles	23.12	28.79	34.24	48.51
30,000 miles	22.38	27.40	32.13	45.03

NB: In the case of diesel cars it is felt that engine size does not adequately reflect the class of car. New purchase price has therefore been used for classification.

Additional notes

The figures only apply with respect to privately owned and used vehicles: they do not apply with respect to company or fleet cars, which frequently attract special discounts in relation to servicing, parts, insurance, etc.

It should also be noted that the figures quoted are averages only and where possible the actual amounts should be substituted. These notes apply to both of the tables.

(a) Road tax — New tax rate introduced from June 1999.

(b) Insurance — Average rates for a fully comprehensive policy with a 60% no-claims allowance.

(c) Depreciation — All cars will depreciate at different rates, depending on make, model, age, mileage, condition, etc. For the purpose of this publication an average annual depreciation figure is calculated and is based on the average cost of a new car within the various engine capacity groups. In the case of second-hand cars, the depreciation should be assessed individually.

(d) Subscription — AA Membership subscription includes Relay.

(e) Petrol/Diesel — Based on the average price of a litre at the time of publication. The cost per mile figure is calculated from what we consider to be a reasonable fuel consumption for the various engine/classification groups.

(f) Engine oil — Allowance is made for normal consumption and routine oil changes.

(g) Tyres — Estimated tyre life of 30,000 miles.

(h) Servicing — Routine servicing as recommended by the vehicle manufacturers. In the case of older motor cars servicing costs may be more.

(i) Repairs and replacements — An allowance is made for routine repairs and replacements which are likely to be needed due to normal wear and tear. However, it is unrealistic for us to allow for any major repairs which will only occur as a result of unexpected mechanical or electrical failures. For this reason, only the owner of the vehicle can assess the true cost of this item, as repair costs will vary, even when comparing identical cars.

Figures for *other periods* and for mopeds, motorcycles and scooters can be obtained from the AA, Technical Services, Lambert House, Stockport Road, Cheadle, Cheshire SK8 2DY (Tel. (0161) 428 7671).

(Reproduced by kind permission of the Automobile Association.)

Mileage allowances: fixed profit car scheme

The tax-free mileage allowances under the fixed profit car scheme, which applies on a voluntary basis to allowances paid by employers to employees who use their own cars for work, are set out below:

	Tax-free rates per mile				
Tax Year	**Cars up to 1,000cc**	**Cars 1,001 to 1,500cc**	**Cars 1,501 to 2,000cc**	**Cars over 2,000cc**	**Composite rate**[1]
1997–98 to 2000–2001					
Up to 4,000 miles	28p	35p	45p	63p	40p
Over 4,000 miles	17p	20p	25p	36p	22.5p
1996–97					
Up to 4,000 miles	27p	34p	43p	61p	38.5p
Over 4,000 miles	16p	19p	23p	33p	21p
1995–96					
Up to 4,000 miles	27p	34p	43p	60p	38.5p
Over 4,000 miles	15p	19p	23p	32p	21p
1994–95					
Up to 4,000 miles	27p	33p	41p	56p	37p
Over 4,000 miles	15p	19p	23p	31p	21p

Notes

[1]Irrespective of engine size.

Transitional arrangements exist (ICTA 1988, s. 197B) to restrict the extent to which tax liabilities on motor mileage allowances can increase from year to year.

Any employee can be taxed individually on the basis of actual motoring expenditure (the statutory basis) if necessary records are kept.

Authorised rate for pedal cycles

Tax year	Tax free rate
1999–2000 to 2000–2001	12p

Authorised rate for motor cycles

Tax year	Tax free rate
2000–2001	24p

Flat rate allowances

Certain taxpayers have a flat-rate deduction for tools, special clothing etc. These are detailed for 1989–90 to 1994–95 and 1995–96 onwards in ESC A1 and Revenue press release 13 February 1981. An employee may claim actual expenditure if he or she can establish that it is greater than the appropriate fixed allowance.

Uniform allowances are available for certain officers of HM Forces.

Income arising outside UK

Income	Residence of individual	Commonwealth citizen with UK domicile	Non-Commonwealth citizen with UK domicile	Non-UK domicile
Income from overseas securities and possessions[1][3]	Resident and ordinarily resident in UK	All taxable	All taxable	Sums remitted to UK taxable
	Resident but not ordinarily resident in UK	Sums remitted to UK taxable[2]	All taxable	Sums remitted to UK taxable
	Non-UK resident	Not taxable	Not taxable	Not taxable
Income from trades and professions carried on and controlled outside UK[1]	Resident and ordinarily resident in UK	All taxable	All taxable	Sums remitted to UK taxable
	Resident but not ordinarily resident in UK	Sums remitted to UK taxable[2]	All taxable	Sums remitted to UK taxable
	Non-UK resident	Not taxable	Not taxable	Not taxable

Notes

[1] The terms of any double tax agreements must be taken into account.

[2] Also applies to citizens of Republic of Ireland.

[3] Foreign pensions, chargeable under Sch. D, Case V, other than those charged on the remittance basis, are taxable subject to a $^1/_{10}$ deduction from the taxable amount (ICTA 1988, s. 65(2)). German and Austrian pensions paid to victims of Nazi persecution are completely non-taxable (ICTA 1988, s. 330).

Foreign employees' liability to UK tax

Earnings	Residence of employee	Earnings from duties performed in UK	Earnings from duties performed partly outside UK	Earnings from duties performed wholly outside UK
Earnings of non-domiciled employee with non-resident employer	Resident and ordinarily resident in UK	All taxable	All taxable	Sums remitted to UK taxable
	Resident but not ordinarily resident in UK	All taxable	Sums remitted to UK taxable	Sums remitted to UK taxable
	Non-UK resident	All taxable	Not taxable	Not taxable
Other earnings	Resident and ordinarily resident in UK	All taxable[1]	All taxable[1]	All taxable[1]
	Resident but not ordinarily resident in UK	All taxable	Sums remitted to UK taxable	Sums remitted to UK taxable
	Non-UK resident	All taxable	Not taxable	Not taxable

Note

[1] Prior to 17 March 1998 the Foreign Earnings Deduction (FED) applied to an individual who spent 365 days or more working outside the UK. The FED was a 100% tax deduction available even if the individual spent no more than $^1/_6$ of the qualifying period in the UK, so long as each individual visit did not exceed 62 days (ICTA 1988, s. 193(1) and Sch. 12). From 17 March 1998 the general FED is abolished, although genuine seafarers will continue to qualify (with extended limits of no more than $^1/_2$ of the qualifying period spent in the UK and single visits restricted to 183 days or less).

Relocation allowance

Statutory relief

(ICTA 1988, s. 191A, 191B and Sch. 11A)

Tax relief for relocation expenses in relation to payments made or expenses provided in connection with an employee's change of residence where the employee's job or place of work is changed is generally subject to a statutory maximum from 6 April 1993. The maximum allowance is:

From	Maximum allowance £
6 April 1993	8,000

Note:

- Tax relief for relocation expenses was given by concession before 6 April 1993 (ESC A5 and A67). The concessionary relief continues to apply if, before 6 April 1993, the employee was firmly committed to move and started work at the new location before 1 August 1993. The maximum amount which may be provided tax free to an employee transferred to a higher-cost housing area from 1 February 1993 is £13,440.

Incidental overnight expenses

(ICTA 1988, s. 200A)

Benefits, reimbursements and expenses provided by an employer for employees' minor, personal expenditure whilst on business-related activities requiring overnight accommodation away from home are not taxable under Sch. E provided that the total amount reimbursed, etc. does not exceed the relevant maximum amount(s) per night, multiplied by the number of nights' absence. If the limit is exceeded the whole amount provided remains taxable.

	Authorised maximum per night	
From	In UK £	Overseas £
6 April 1995	5	10

Payroll giving scheme

(ICTA 1988, s. 202)

Employees whose remuneration is subject to deduction of tax at source under PAYE can make donations to charity by requesting that their employers deduct the donations from their pay.

Year	Maximum donation per year £
1996–97 to 1999–2000	1,200
1993–94 to 1995–96	900

Notes

The £1,200 ceiling on payroll giving is abolished from 2000–2001.

The £250 minimum limit for donations under the Gift Aid scheme is abolished from 6 April 2000.

The Government will provide a 10% supplement on all payroll giving donations until April 2003.

Small maintenance payments

(ICTA 1988, s. 351; FA 1988, s. 37–40)

	Payments due after 5 April 1986	
Payment made:	**Monthly £**	**Weekly £**
by one of the parties to a marriage (including a marriage which has been annulled or dissolved) to or for the benefit of the other party to that marriage for that other party's maintenance	208	48
to any person under 21 years of age for his own benefit maintenance or education	208	48
to any person for the benefit maintenance or education of a person under 21 years of age	108	25

Notes

Relief for maintenance payments is withdrawn generally from 6 April 2000 (FA 1999, s. 36).

Relief continues where either party to the marriage was born before 6 April 1935. In such cases, relief is given under the rules relating to post 15 March 1988 arrangements.

The payer will obtain relief on the first £1,900 restricted to 15% for 1998–99 and 10% for 1999–2000.

Since 5 April 1989 all maintenance payments should have been made gross.

The new rules for maintenance payments do *not* apply to payments made after 5 April 1988 under:

- court orders made before 15 March 1988;
- court orders applied for on or before 15 March 1988 and made by 30 June 1988 and maintenance agreements made before 15 March 1988 provided that a copy of the agreement was received by the Revenue by 30 June 1988;
- court orders or agreements made on or after 15 March 1988 which vary or replace such orders or agreements.

After 1988–89 the payer obtains relief on payments up to the level for which he obtained relief for 1988–89 and the recipient is taxable on an amount not exceeding the amount which was taxable in 1988–89. Since 1994, the relief is restricted by treating an amount equal to the current year's married couple's allowance as if it were a qualifying maintenance payment under the post-1988 rules.

For details of previous years' reliefs and restrictions, see p. 2 for the married couple's allowance figures to which maintainance payments are linked.

Individual Savings Accounts (ISAs)

(ICTA 1988, s. 333)

ISAs start on 6 April 1999 and are guaranteed to run to at least 5 April 2009.

	Maximum investment per year
	1999–2000 and 2001–2001 **£**
Maxi ISA	7,000
made up of:	
Stocks and shares	up to 7,000
Cash	up to 3,000
Life insurance	up to 1,000
Mini ISA types:	
Stocks and shares	3,000
Cash	3,000
Life insurance	1,000

Notes

- A Maxi ISA can include a stocks and shares component, cash component and a life insurance component in a single ISA with one manager. Mini ISAs are separate ISAs, from different managers, for stocks and shares, cash and life insurance.
- Each year an individual can either start new ISAs or can put money into existing ISAs, but only into one Maxi ISA, or one Mini ISA of each type, in any particular tax year.
- To open an ISA an individual has to be aged 18 or over and resident and ordinarily resident in the UK for tax purposes.
- All income and gains derived from investments and life assurance policies within the account are tax free and withdrawals from the account will not attract any tax charge.
- Tax credits attached to dividends from UK companies (which from 6 April 1999 have a value of 10%) are to be paid into the ISA until 5 April 2004. There is a similar entitlement until 5 April 2004 to tax credits attached to dividends which derive from UK equities which back life assurance policies within an ISA. The life assurance company will be able to claim payment of such tax credits.
- On maturity after 5 April 1999, the capital element of a TESSA may be transferred into the cash component of an ISA. Neither the value of any TESSA held, nor the amount of any transfer on maturity, will affect the amount which can be subscribed to an ISA.
- All Personal Equity Plans (PEPs) held at 5 April 1999 can continue to be held as PEPs, but with the same tax advantages as ISAs. Tax-exempt Special Savings Accounts (TESSAs) which were open at 5 April 1999 can continue to be paid into under existing rules for their full five-year life. After that date, capital from maturing TESSAs can be transferred into the cash component of an ISA.

Settlements on children

(ICTA 1988, s. 663(4))

Income paid to or for the benefit of a minor child arising from capital provided by a parent is not treated as parents' income if it does not exceed £100 per tax year.

Enterprise investment scheme (EIS)

(ICTA 1988, s. 289–312)

The EIS applies for 1993–94 and subsequent tax years and is effective in relation to shares issued after 31 December 1993.

Relief on investment	From	Amount
Maximum	1998–99 1994–95 1993–94	£150,000 £100,000 £40,000[1]
Minimum investment	1993–94	£500
Maximum carry-back to preceding year on investments made between 6 April and 5 October	1998–99	The lower of: • 50% of the total relief in respect of the investments; and • £25,000 (£15,000 for 1994–95 to 1997–98)
Rate of relief on income tax	1993–94	20%

Notes
[1] Applied to an individual's combined investment under the business expansion scheme and the enterprise investment scheme.

The first disposal of shares on which relief has not been withdrawn is exempt from capital gains tax; losses arising from the first disposal of shares are eligible for relief against either income tax or capital gains tax.
Reinvestment relief is available for gains on assets where the disposal proceeds are reinvested in new EIS shares.
Under TCGA 1992, Sch. 5BA, taper relief will be given for the gain on the first investment as though it had been owned throughout the period during which the investor remains invested in EIS companies.

Venture capital trusts (VCTs)

(ICTA 1988, s. 332A, 842AA, Sch. 15B; TCGA 1992, s. 151A, 151B, Sch. 5C)

A VCT is a type of investment trust, approved by the Revenue on or after 6 April 1995.

Reliefs:

- income tax relief of 20% on up to £100,000 per tax year subscribed for new ordinary shares in VCTs is available if the shares are held for five years;
- investors will not be taxed on dividends received from VCTs provided they are within the investment limit exempt from higher rate income tax;
- if an individual disposes of shares in a VCT the gain will be exempt from capital gains tax if the acquisition cost of the shares did not exceed £100,000 in any one year and the shares were held for five years; and
- individuals who subscribe for new ordinary shares in a VCT, on which they have been given income tax relief, will be able to defer CGT on a chargeable gain which arises from the disposal of any assets where the gain is reinvested in the new ordinary shares within the period from one year before, to one year after, the date on which the gain arises.

To obtain the Revenue's approval the trust must satisfy certain conditions. The main ones are as follows:

- it must be a non-close company;
- its shares must be quoted on the stock exchange;
- at least 70% of its income must be wholly or mainly derived from investments in shares or securities; and
- at least 70% (by value) of its total investments must comprise 'qualifying holdings' (broadly, shares in unquoted trading companies).

Gilt-edged securities held by non-residents (FOTRA securities)

With effect from 6 April 1998, interest on all gilt-edged securities is payable gross (F(No. 2)A 1997, s. 37). Interest on gilts already in issue at that date which is payable under deduction of tax will continue to be payable net unless notice is given to the Bank of England for payment to be made gross. Interest on gilts issued since 5 April 1998 may be paid net, if the holder wishes, again by notice to the Bank of England. Payment gross does not of itself imply that the interest is exempt from tax.

Prior to 6 April 1998, certain specified gilts, and the interest payable on them, were exempt from all UK taxation as long as it was shown that they were in the beneficial ownership of persons who were not ordinarily resident in the UK (so called FOTRA gilts). If interest was payable under deduction of tax, that tax could be reclaimed without recourse to the terms of any applicable double tax treaty. A list of such FOTRA gilts is provided in the table below (excluding securities which have been redeemed).

With effect from 6 April 1998, *all* gilt-edged securities will automatically be given FOTRA status, thereby guaranteeing exemption from tax for holders not ordinarily resident in the UK.

Description

Security	Date(s) for repayment
9% Conversion Stock 2000	3 March 2000
9% Conversion Stock 2011	12 July 2011
9½% Conversion Stock 2001	12 July 2001
9¾% Conversion Stock 2003	7 May 2003
Floating Rate Treasury Stock 1999	9 March 1999(1)
Floating Rate Treasury Stock 2001	8 July 2001
2½% Index Linked Treasury Stock 2024	Not later than 17 July 2024
4⅛% Index Linked Treasury Stock 2030	22 July 2030
4⅜% Index Linked Treasury Stock 2004	21 October 2004
4⅝% Index Linked Treasury Stock 1998	27 April 1998
5½% Treasury Stock 2008/12	10 September 2008 to 10 September 2012
6% Treasury Stock 1999	10 August 1999
6% Treasury Stock 2028	7 December 2028
6¼% Treasury Stock 2010	25 November 2010
6½% Treasury Loan 2003	7 December 2003
6¾% Treasury Loan 2004	26 November 2004
7% Treasury Stock 2001	6 November 2001
7% Treasury Stock 2002	7 June 2002
7¼% Treasury Stock 2007	7 December 2007
7½% Treasury Stock 2006	7 December 2006
7¾% Treasury Stock 2006	8 September 2006
7¾% Treasury Loan 2012/15	26 January 2012 to 26 January 2015
8% Treasury Stock 2000	7 December 2000
8% Treasury Loan 2002/06	5 October 2002 to 5 October 2006
8% Treasury Stock 2003	10 June 2003
8% Treasury Stock 2013	27 September 2013
8% Treasury Stock 2015	7 December 2015
8% Treasury Stock 2021	7 June 2021
8½% Treasury Loan 2000	28 January 2000
8½% Treasury Stock 2005	7 December 2005
8½% Treasury Loan 2007	16 July 2007
8¾% Treasury Loan 2017	25 August 2017
9% Treasury Loan 2008	13 October 2008
9% Treasury Stock 2012	6 August 2012
9½% Treasury Loan 1999	15 January 1999
15½% Treasury Loan 1998	30 September 1998
3½% War Loan	

Notes

(1) Interest is paid by the Bank of England without deduction of UK income tax.

List prepared by FICO (International), Fitz Roy House, PO Box 46, Castle Meadow Road, Nottingham, NG2 1BD.

Official rates of interest (beneficial loan arrangements)

(ICTA 1988, s. 160)

Where an employee or a director earning £8,500 or more a year has outstanding for the whole or part of a year a loan obtained by reason of employment, and no interest or a lesser amount than the official rate is paid for that year, then the cash equivalent is to be treated as an emolument of the employment chargeable to tax under Sch. E.

Period of application		Rate %
From 6 March 1999		6.25
6 August 1997 to	5 March 1999	7.25
6 November 1996 to	5 August 1997	6.75
6 June 1996 to	5 November 1996	7
6 February 1996 to	5 June 1996	7.25
6 October 1995 to	5 February 1996	7.75
6 November 1994 to	5 October 1995	8
6 January 1994 to	5 November 1994	7.5
6 March 1993 to	5 January 1994	7.75

Notes

From 6 April 1994:

- there is no tax charge if all the employee's cheap or interest-free loans total no more than £5,000; or
- where the employee's cheap or interest-free loans total more than £5,000, there is no tax charge in respect of 'non-qualifying' loans totailing no more than £5,000.

A 'non-qualifying' loan is one in respect of which interest paid does not qualify for relief under ICTA 1988, s. 353 (ignoring the exclusion of MIRAS loans) and is disallowed in computing the charge under Sch. D, Cases I and II.

Prior to 6 April 1994 there is no charge to income tax if the benefit in respect of a cheap or interest-free loan is £300 p.a. or less.

Foreign currency loans

A lower 'official rate' of interest for taxing loans in a foreign currency is set where interest rates in that country are significantly lower than interest rates in the UK. This relief will only apply to a loan in another country's currency, to a person who normally lives in that country and has actually lived there in the year or previous five years. Lower rates of interest for loans in Japanese yen or Swiss francs have been set as follows:

Loans in Swiss francs	
Date	**Rate %**
From 6 July 1994	5.5
From 6 June 1994 to 5 July 1994	5.7
Loans in Japanese yen	
Date	**Rate %**
From 6 June 1994	3.9

Time limits for elections and claims

In the absence of any provision to the contrary, under self-assessment for the purposes of income tax, the normal rule is that claims are to be made within five years from 31 January next following the tax year to which they relate, previously six years from the end of the relevant chargeable period (TMA 1970, s. 43(1)).

For details of time limits relating to payment of tax, see pp. 9, 47, 92 and 97.

In certain cases the Board *may* permit an extension of the strict time limit in relation to certain elections and claims.

Provision	**Time limit**	**Statutory reference**
Actual basis of assessment in second and third years of a trade (pre current-year basis)	7 years from end of the second tax year	ICTA 1988, s. 62(2)
Actual basis of assessment in fifth and sixth years of a partnership (pre current-year basis)	7 years from end of the fifth tax year	ICTA 1988, s. 62(4)
Actual basis of assessment in third year of a Sch. D, Case III–V source (or second year if income first arose on 6 April) (pre current-year basis)	6 years from end of tax year	ICTA 1988, s. 66(1)(c)
Averaging of farmers' profits	12 months from 31 January next following end of the second tax year concerned	ICTA 1988, s. 96(8)
Stock transferred to a connected party on cessation of trade to be valued at higher of cost or sale price	2 years from end of chargeable period in which trade ceased	ICTA 1988, s. 100(1C)
Post-cessation expenses relieved against income and chargeable gains	12 months from 31 January next following that year from 1996–97 (previously 2 years from end of tax year)	ICTA 1988, s. 109A
Continuation basis of assessment for partnership (prior to self-assessment)	2 years from date of partnership change	ICTA 1988, s. 113(2)
Elections for transfer of married couple's allowance	Generally before the first tax year for which it is to have effect, and before end of year of marriage	ICTA 1988, s. 257BA(4)
Transfer of excess married couple's allowance to wife	5 years from 31 January next following tax year to which it relates from 1996–97 (previously 6 years from end of tax year)	ICTA 1988, s. 257BB(5)
Transfer of husband's unutilised personal allowances to wife		ICTA 1988, s. 257D
Election for split of income from investments	Send to Revenue within 60 days of effective date	ICTA 1988, s. 282B(3)
Allocation of mortgage interest	12 months from 31 January next following the first tax year for which election is made or such later date as the Board may allow from 1996–97 (previously 12 months from end of tax year) (see SP 8/89)	ICTA 1988, s. 356B(2), (4)

Provision	Time limit	Statutory reference
Current and preceding year set-off of trading losses	12 months from 31 January next following tax year loss arose from 1996–97 (previously 2 years from end of tax year in which loss is used for set off against current and following year)	ICTA 1988, s. 380(1), (2); FA 1991, s. 72
Three-year carry-back of trading losses in opening years of trade	12 months from 31 January next following tax year loss arose from 1996–97 (previously 2 years from end of tax year)	ICTA 1988, s. 381(1)
Carry-forward of trading losses	5 years from 31 January next following tax year in which loss arose from 1996–97 (previously 6 years from end of tax year in which loss arose)	ICTA 1988, s. 385(1)
Carry-back of terminal losses	5 years from 31 January next following tax year from 1996–97 (previously 6 years from end of tax year)	ICTA 1988, s. 388(1)
Set-off of loss on disposal of shares in unquoted trading company against income	12 months from 31 January following year in which loss arose from 1996–97 (previously 2 years from end of tax year)	ICTA 1988, s. 574(1)
Carry-back of retirement annuity premiums	31 January next following tax year in which paid from 1996–97 (previously before end of tax year in which paid – in practice limit extended to next 5 July)	ICTA 1988, s. 619(4)
Carry-back of personal pension scheme contributions	31 January next following tax year in which paid from 1996–97 (previously 3 months from end of tax year in which paid)	ICTA 1988, s. 641(1), (4)
Certain plant and machinery treated as 'short life' assets	12 months from 31 January next following the tax year in which ends the chargeable period related to the incurring of the capital expenditure from 1996–97 (previously 2 years from end of chargeable/basis period)	CAA 1990, s. 37(2)
Transfer between connected parties of certain assets, eligible for capital allowances, at tax-written down value	2 years from date of sale (for sales after 29 July 1988)	CAA 1990, s. 158(1)

National Savings Bank interest

Limit of income tax exemption under ICTA 1988, s. 325 (all years since 1977–78): £70. The exemption is available in respect of separate accounts of husband and wife. The exemption is unavailable in respect of investment deposits.

Statutory sick pay

Employers are liable to pay SSP in any period of incapacity to work to a maximum of 28 weeks at the SSP rate in force. Statutory sick pay is treated as wages and is subject to PAYE income tax and to National Insurance contributions. Statutory sick pay is not payable for certain periods in which statutory maternity pay is being paid.

The amount of SSP payable to an employee depends on the earnings band into which he or she falls. The earnings bands and the associated SSP payments are as follows:

Year to	Average gross weekly earnings £	Weekly SSP rate £
5 April 2001	67.00 or more	60.20
5 April 2000	66.00 or more	59.55
5 April 1999	64.00 or more	57.70
5 April 1998	62.00 or more	55.70
5 April 1997	61.00 or more	54.55
5 April 1996	58.00 or more	52.50
5 April 1995	200.00 or more	52.50
	57.00–199.99	47.80

Maximum entitlement

An employee reaches his maximum entitlement to SSP in one spell of incapacity when he has been paid 28 times the appropriate rate, i.e. £60.20 × 28 = £1,685.60.

Statutory maternity pay

Higher weekly rate:(1)	$^9/_{10}$ of employee's average weekly earnings	
Lower weekly rate:(2)	from 6 April 2000	£60.20
	from 6 April 1999	£59.55
	from 6 April 1998	£57.70
	from 6 April 1997	£55.70
	from 7 April 1996	£54.55
	from 16 October 1994	£52.50
	from 6 April 1994	£48.80

Notes

(1) Payable for the first six weeks of payment.

(2) Payable for the remaining weeks of the Maternity Pay Period.

Taxable state benefits

The following benefits are liable to income tax (ICTA 1988, s. 617):

Benefit	Weekly rate from 10 April 2000 £	Weekly rate from 12 April 1999 £
Industrial death benefit:		
Widow's pension		
Permanent rate — higher	67.50	66.75
lower	20.25	20.03
Invalid care allowance		
Standard rate	40.40	39.95
Incapacity benefit (long term)		
Rate	67.50	66.75
Increase for age:		
higher rate	14.20	14.05
lower rate	7.10	7.05
Incapacity benefit (short term)		
Higher rate:		
under pensionable age[(1)]	60.20	59.55
over pensionable age[(1)]	67.50	66.75
Non-contributory retirement pension		
Standard rate	40.40	39.95
Age addition (at age 80)	0.25	0.25
Retirement pension		
Standard rate	67.50	66.75
Age addition (at age 80)	0.25	0.25
Jobseeker's allowance		
See p. 37		
SSP and SMP		
See pp. 33		
Widow's benefit[(2)]		
Pension (standard rate)	67.50	66.75
Widowed mother's allowance	67.50	66.75
Dependent adults		
with retirement pension	40.40	39.95
with invalid care allowance	24.15	23.90
Hospital down rating		
20% rate	13.50	13.35
40% rate	27.00	26.70

Notes

(1) Pensionable age is 60 for women, 65 for men. From 6 April 2020 the state pension age for women will be 65, the same as for men. From 2010 women's state pension age will be gradually increased to bring it up to age 65 by 2020.

(2) Widow's payment (lump sum) is £1,000, which is non taxable.

State benefits: not taxable

The following benefits are not liable to income tax:

- Attendance allowance
- Back to work bonus
- Child benefit
- Child maintenance bonus
- Christmas bonus
- Constant attendance allowance
- Council tax benefit
- Council tax benefit extended payment
- Criminal injuries compensation
- Disability living allowance
- Education welfare benefits
- Employment rehabilitation allowance
- Guardian's allowance
- Housing benefit
- Housing benefit extended payment
- Incapacity benefit (short-term–lower rate)
- Income support
- Industrial injuries disablement benefit
- Jobseeker's allowance, amounts above personal or couple rate
- Lone parent's benefit run-on
- Maternity allowance
- Medical expenses incurred in the European Economic Area
- Motability
- Pneumoconiosis, byssinosis and misc. disease scheme benefits
- Reduced earnings allowance
- Statutory redundancy payments
- Retirement allowance (payable under industrial injuries scheme)
- Severe disablement allowance
- Social fund payments – budgeting loan, cold weather payment, community care grant, crisis loan, funeral payment, maternity payment, winter fuel payments
- Vaccine damage
- War disablement pension
- War pensioner's mobility supplement
- War widow's pension
- Widow's payment
- Widowed mother's allowance child dependency increase
- Worker's compensation (supplementation) scheme

Benefit	Weekly rate (£)	
Attendance allowance	**from 10 April 2000**	**from 12 April 1999**
Higher rate (day and night)	53.55	52.95
Lower rate (day or night)	35.80	35.40
Child benefit		
For the eldest qualifying child	15.00	14.40
Lone parent	17.55	17.10
For each other child	10.00	9.60
Christmas bonus		
Single annual payment	10.00	10.00
Constant attendance allowance		
Exceptional rate	87.60	86.60
Intermediate rate	65.70	64.95
Normal maximum rate	43.80	43.30
Maternity allowance		
Lower rate	52.25	51.70
Higher rate	60.20	59.55
Guardian's allowance[1]		
Eldest qualifying child	9.85	9.90
Each other child	11.35	11.35
Disability living allowance (care component)		
Higher rate	53.55	52.95
Middle rate	35.80	35.40
Lower rate	14.20	14.05
Disability living allowance (mobility component)		
Higher rate	37.40	37.00
Lower rate	14.20	14.05
Income support **see p. 37**		
Severe disablement allowance		
Basic rate	40.80	40.35
There are additions related to the age of becoming incapable of work:		
under 40	14.20	14.05
under 50	9.00	8.90
under 60	4.50	4.45
Extra benefit for dependent adult over pensionable age[3]	24.20	23.95
Incapacity benefit (short term)[4]		
Lower rate:		
under pensionable age[3]	50.90	50.35
over pensionable age[3]	64.75	64.05

Notes

[1] Also child special allowance, and child dependency increases with retirement pension, widow's benefit, short-term incapacity benefit at the higher rate and long-term incapacity benefit, invalid care allowance, severe disablement allowance, higher rate individual death benefit, unemployability supplement and short-term incapacity benefit if beneficiary over pension age.

[2] Incapacity benefit replaced invalidity benefit and sickness benefit from 6 April 1995. It is taxable, under Sch. E, except for short-term benefit payable at the lower rate.

[3] Pensionable age is 60 for women, 65 for men. From 6 April 2020 the state pension age for women will be 65, the same as for men. From 2010 women's state pension age will be gradually increased to bring it up to age 65 by 2020.

Income support and jobseeker's allowance

Income support is not taxable.

The personal or couple rate of jobseeker's allowance is taxable. Any amounts of jobseeker's allowance payable above the personal or couple rate (e.g. premiums) are not taxable.

Rate of income support

Single	Weekly rate from 10 April 2000 £	Weekly rate from 12 April 1999 £
Aged 16 to 17	31.45	30.95
Aged 16 to 17 (higher rate)	41.35	40.70
Aged 18 to 24		
Aged 25 and over	41.35	40.70
Couple		
Both aged 16 to 17	62.35	61.35
One aged 18 and over	81.95	80.65
Lone parent		
Aged 16 to 17	31.45	30.95
Aged 16 to 17 (higher rate)	41.35	40.70
Aged 18 and over	52.20	51.40
Dependent children		
From birth to age 11[1]	26.60	24.90
Age 11 to 16[2]	26.60	25.90
Age 16 to 19[3]	31.75	30.95

Notes

[1] From birth to first Sunday in September following 11th birthday.

[2] From first Monday in September following 11th birthday to first Sunday in September following 16th birthday.

[3] From first Monday in September following 16th birthday to the day before 19th birthday.

Rates of jobseeker's allowance

	Weekly rate £	
	From 10 April 2000	From 12 April 1999
Contribution based JSA, personal allowance		
Aged under 18	31.45	30.95
Aged 18 to 24	41.35	40.70
Aged 25 and over	52.20	51.40
Income based JSA, personal allowance[4]		
Aged under 18	31.45	30.95
Aged 18 to 24	41.35	40.70
Aged 25 and over	52.20	51.40
Couple		
Both under 18	31.45	30.95
Both under 18, one disabled	41.35	40.70
Both under 18, with responsibility for a child	62.35	61.35
One under 18, one 18 to 24	41.35	40.70
One under 18, one 25 or over	52.20	51.40
Both 18 or over	81.95	80.60
Dependent children[5]		
From birth to age 11	26.60	24.90
Age 11 to 16	26.60	25.90
Age 16 to 19	31.75	30.95

Notes

[4] Also lone parent rate.

[5] See footnotes 1 to 3 under Rates of Income Support.

Income support and jobseeker's allowance – premiums

Premium	Weekly rate from 10 April 2000 £	Weekly rate from 12 April 1999 £
Family	14.25	13.90
Family (lone parent rate)	15.90	15.75
Pensioner (single)	26.25	23.60
Pensioner (couple)	40.00	35.95
Pensioner (enhanced) – single		25.90
Pensioner (enhanced) – couple	43.40	39.20
Pensioner (higher) – single	33.85	30.85
Pensioner (higher) – couple	49.10	44.65
Disability – single	22.25	21.90
Disability – couple	31.75	31.25
Severe disability – single	40.20	39.75
Severe disability – couple (one qualifies)	40.20	39.75
Severe disability – couple (both qualify)	80.40	79.50
Disabled child	22.25	21.90
Carer	14.15	13.95

NATIONAL INSURANCE CONTRIBUTIONS

Class 1 contributions

Class 1 primary (employee) contributions 2000–2001[1]	
Lower earnings limit (LEL)[2]	£67 weekly £291 monthly £3,484 yearly
Primary threshold	£76 weekly £329 monthly £3,952 yearly
Rate on earnings up to primary threshold	0%
Not contracted-out rate on earnings between primary threshold and upper earnings limit (UEL)	10%
Contracted-out rate on earnings between primary threshold and upper earnings limit (UEL)	8.4%
Reduced rate on earnings between primary threshold and UEL[3]	3.85%
Upper earnings limit	£535 weekly £2,319 monthly £27,820 yearly

Notes

[1] Class 1 contributions are earnings related. Employees must pay primary Class 1 contributions on that part of their earnings which exceeds the primary threshold, up to the upper earnings limit.

[2] Earnings up to and including the lower earnings limit (LEL) for 1999–2000 and later years will count towards the employee's basic 'flat rate' state pension, even though no contributions will have been paid on those earnings. Similarly, earnings between the LEL and the primary threshold will count towards the employee's entitlement to certain benefits including the additional pension (SERPS).

[3] The reduced rate applies to married women or widows with a valid certificate of election. Men over 65 and women over 60 pay no primary contributions, though employers still pay the secondary contribution at the usual rate. People under 16 and their employers pay no contributions.

Class 1 secondary (employer) contributions 2000–2001[4]	
Earnings threshold	£84 weekly £365 monthly £4,385 yearly
Not contracted-out rate	12.2% above earnings threshold
Contracted-out rates[5]	9.2% for salary-related (COSR) and 11.6% for money-purchase (COMP) schemes (including 3% and 0.6% rebates for earnings from LEL to earnings threshold), then 12.2% above UEL[6].

Notes

[4] Class 1 contributions are earnings related. Employers must pay secondary Class 1 contributions on that part of an employee's earnings which exceeds the earnings threshold, without limit (i.e. without capping).

[5] With contracted-out salary related (COSR) schemes there is an employer's NIC rebate of 3% of earnings above the employer's earnings threshold, up to and including the upper earnings limit. With contracted-out money purchase (COMP) schemes there is an employer's NIC rebate of 0.6% of earnings above the employer's earnings threshold, up to and including the upper earnings limit, and a further age-related rebate is paid by the Inland Revenue National Insurance Contributions Office directly to the scheme (see table at p. 42).

[6] For UEL (upper earnings limit) see p. 40.

Class 1 contributions (1999–2000): not contracted-out[1]

Earnings brackets	Employee		Employer
	Standard	Reduced[2]	All earnings
£0.00 to £66.00[3] weekly or £0.00 to £286.00 monthly or £0.00 to £3,432.00 yearly	Nil	Nil	Nil
£66.01 to £83.00[4] weekly or £286.01 to £361.00 monthly or £3,432.01 to £4,335.00 yearly	10% on earnings above the LEL	3.85% on earnings above the LEL	Nil
£83.01 to £500.00[5] weekly or £361.01 to £2,167.00 monthly or £4,335.01 to £26,000.00 yearly	10% on earnings above the LEL	3.85% on earnings above the LEL	12.2% on earnings above the earnings threshold
Over £500.00 weekly or over £2,167.00 monthly or over £26,000.00 yearly	10% on earnings above the LEL up to and including the UEL	3.85% on earnings above the LEL up to and including the UEL	12.2% on all earnings above the earnings threshold

Notes

(1) Class 1 contributions are earnings related. Employees must pay Class 1 contributions if their earnings reach the lower earnings limit (LEL). Employee's (primary) contributions are paid on all earnings up to an upper earnings limit (UEL). Employer's (secondary) contributions are paid on all of an employee's earnings above an earnings threshold (which is linked with the personal tax allowance).

(2) The reduced rate applies to married women or widows with a valid certificate of election. Men over 65 and women over 60 pay no primary contributions, though employers still pay the secondary contribution at the usual rate. People under 16 and their employers pay no contributions.

(3) £66.00 a week, or its monthly or yearly equivalent shown in this box, is the lower earnings limit (LEL) for 1999–2000.

(4) £83.00 a week, or its monthly or yearly equivalent shown in this box, is the earnings threshold for 1999–2000.

(5) £500.00 a week, or its monthly or yearly equivalent shown in this box, is the upper earnings limit (UEL) for 1999–2000.

Class 1 contributions (1999–2000): contracted-out[1]

Earnings brackets	Employees		Employers	
	Standard	Reduced[2]	COSR[3]	COMP[4]
£0.00 to £66.00[5] weekly or £0.00 to £286.00 monthly or £0.00 to £3,432.00 yearly	Nil	Nil	Nil	Nil
£66.01 to £83.00[6] weekly or £286.01 to £361.00 monthly or £3,432.01 to £4,335.00 yearly	8.4% on earnings above the LEL	3.85% on earnings above the LEL	Nil[7]	Nil[8]
£83.01 to £500.00[9] weekly or £361.01 to £2,167.00 monthly or £4,335.01 to £26,000.00 yearly	8.4% on earnings above the LEL	3.85% on earnings above the LEL	9.2% on earnings above the earnings threshold	11.6% on earnings above the earnings threshold[10]
Over £500.00 weekly or over £2,167.00 monthly or over £26,000.00 yearly	8.4% on earnings above the LEL up to and including the UEL	3.85% on earnings above the LEL up to and including the UEL	9.2% on earnings above the earnings threshold, up to and including the UEL, then 12.2% on all earnings above the UEL	11.6% on earnings above the earnings threshold, up to and including the UEL, then 12.2% on all earnings above the UEL

Notes

(1) Class 1 contributions are earnings related. Employees must pay Class 1 contributions if their earnings reach the lower earnings limit (LEL). Employee's (primary) contributions are paid on all earnings up to an upper earnings limit (UEL). Employer's (secondary) contributions are paid on all of an employee's earnings above an earnings threshold (which is linked with the personal tax allowance).

(2) The reduced rate applies to married women or widows with a valid certificate of election. Men over 65 and women over 60 pay no primary contributions, though employers still pay the secondary contribution at the usual rate. People under 16 and their employers pay no contributions.

(3) Employer operates a contracted-out salary related (COSR) scheme.

(4) Employer operates a contracted-out money purchase (COMP) scheme.

(5) £66.00 a week, or its monthly or yearly equivalent shown in this box, is the lower earnings limit (LEL) for 1999–2000.

(6) £83.00 a week, or its monthly or yearly equivalent shown in this box, is the earnings threshold for 1999–2000.

(7) With COSR schemes there is an employer's NIC rebate of 3% of earnings above the LEL, up to and including the earnings threshold.

(8) With COMP schemes there is an employer's NIC rebate of 0.6% of earnings above the LEL, up to and including the earnings threshold.

(9) £500.00 a week, or its monthly or yearly equivalent shown in this box, is the upper earnings limit (UEL) for 1999–2000.

(10) A further age-related rebate is paid by the Contributions Agency directly to the scheme (see table at p. 42).

Class 1 contracted-out rebates 1999–2000 to 2001–02

Flat-rate rebate

	COSR (salary related) %	COMP (money purchase) %
Employees	1.6	1.6
Employers	3	0.6 + age-related percentage (see table at p. 42)

TABLE

Appropriate age-related percentages of earnings exceeding the lower earnings limit but not the upper earnings limit.

Age on last day of preceding tax year	Appropriate age-related percentages for the tax year		
	1999-2000	2000-01	2001-02
15	2.2	2.2	2.2
16	2.2	2.2	2.2
17	2.3	2.3	2.3
18	2.3	2.3	2.3
19	2.3	2.4	2.4
20	2.4	2.4	2.4
21	2.5	2.5	2.5
22	2.5	2.5	2.5
23	2.6	2.6	2.6
24	2.6	2.6	2.6
25	2.7	2.7	2.7
26	2.7	2.7	2.7
27	2.8	2.8	2.8
28	2.9	2.9	2.9
29	2.9	2.9	2.9
30	3.0	3.0	3.0
31	3.0	3.0	3.0
32	3.1	3.1	3.1
33	3.2	3.2	3.2
34	3.2	3.2	3.3
35	3.3	3.3	3.3
36	3.4	3.4	3.4
37	3.5	3.5	3.5
38	3.7	3.6	3.5
39	3.8	3.8	3.7
40	4.0	3.9	3.8
41	4.2	4.1	4.0
42	4.4	4.3	4.2
43	4.6	4.5	4.4
44	5.0	4.7	4.6
45	5.6	5.1	4.8
46	6.3	5.7	5.2
47	7.1	6.4	5.8
48	8.0	7.2	6.6
49	8.8	8.2	7.4
50	9.0	9.0	8.4
51	9.0	9.0	9.0
52	9.0	9.0	9.0
53	9.0	9.0	9.0
54	9.0	9.0	9.0
55	9.0	9.0	9.0
56	9.0	9.0	9.0
57	9.0	9.0	9.0
58	9.0	9.0	9.0
59	9.0	9.0	9.0
60	9.0	9.0	9.0
61	9.0	9.0	9.0
62	9.0	9.0	9.0
63	9.0	9.0	9.0

Class 1A contributions

From 5 April 1991 employers (but not employees) pay NICs on an annual basis on cars or fuel provided for the private use of employees earning at the rate of £8,500 pa or more or for directors. The liability is calculated on the income tax car and fuel scale rates (see p. 16). From 6 April 2000, employers (but not employees) pay NICs on an annual basis on benefits in kind provided to employees earning at the rate of £8,500 pa or more or to directors. The Class 1A rate for 2000–2001 is 12.2 per cent. Contributions for the year 1999–2000 are due on 19 July 2000.

Return deadlines for Class 1 and 1A contributions

Forms	Date	Penalty provision
End of year returns P14, P35, P38 and P38A	19 May following year of assessment	TMA 1970, s. 98A

Notes

In cases of PAYE and NIC default there are provisions to prevent double charging.

Class 1A contributions are recorded annually in arrears. Penalties will only be imposed if there is a delay in the submission of the relevant year's PAYE return.

Rate of Class 1B contributions

From 6 April 1999 Class 1B contributions are payable by employers on the amount of emoluments in a PAYE settlement agreement which are chargeable to Class 1 or Class 1A NICs, together with the total amount of income tax payable under the agreement. Class 1B contributions are charged at a rate equal to the secondary rate of NICs (12.2 per cent in 2000–2001), with power for the Secretary of State to alter the rate by statutory instrument; but not so as to increase it to more than two per cent above the rate applicable at the end of the preceding year.

Class 2 contributions

Tax year	Weekly contribution: Normal rate £	Weekly contribution: Share fishermen £	Weekly contribution: Volunteer development workers £	Small earnings exception limit £
2000–2001	2.00	2.65	3.35	3,825
1999–2000	6.55	7.20	3.30	3,770
1998–99	6.35	7.00	3.20	3,590
1997–98	6.15	6.80	3.10	3,480
1996–97	6.05	7.20	3.05	3,430
1995–96	5.75	7.30	2.90	3,260
1994–95	5.65	7.75	3.19	3,200

Class 3 contributions

Tax year	Weekly contribution £
2000–2001	6.55
1999–2000	6.45
1998–99	6.25
1997–98	6.05
1996–97	5.95
1995–96	5.65
1994–95	5.55

Class 4 contributions

Tax year	Percentage rate %	Annual lower earnings limit £	Annual upper earnings limit £	Maximum contribution £
2000–2001	7.0	4,385	27,820	1,640.45
1999–2000	6.0	7,530	26,000	1,108.20
1998–99	6.0	7,310	25,220	1,074.60
1997–98	6.0	7,010	24,180	1,030.20
1996–97	6.0	6,860	23,660	1,008.00
1995–96	7.3	6,640	22,880	1,185.52
1994–95	7.3	6,490	22,360	1,158.51
1993–94	6.3	6,340	21,840	976.50

Note
For years before 1996–97, Class 4 contributions are 50% income tax deductible.

Interest on Class 1, 1A, 1B and 4 contributions

Interest on late payments of Class 1 and 1A contributions was introduced with effect from 19 April 1993 for 1992–93 and subsequent tax years (*Social Security Contributions and Benefits Act* 1992, Sch. 1, para. 6(2) and (3)). Interest on late payment of Class 1B contributions was introduced with effect from 6 April 1999 for 1998–99 and subsequent tax years. Interest is charged on Class 1 contributions unpaid 14 days after the end of the tax year in which they were due and on Class 1A contributions unpaid 14 days after the end of the tax year in which they were due to be paid. Interest is charged on Class 1B contributions unpaid by 19 October following the tax year for which they are payable. See p. 64.

For assessments issued after 18 April 1993 interest can be charged on overdue Class 4 contributions at the prescribed rate (see p. 64).

Interest is paid on repayments of overpaid Class 1, 1A, 1B and 4 contributions from the dates shown above until repayment (see p. 66).

CORPORATION TAX

Corporation tax rates

Financial year	Full rate %	Small companies' rate %	Profit limit for small companies' rate (lower limit)	Profit limit for small companies' marginal relief (upper limit)	Marginal relief fraction for small companies	Starting rate %	Profit limit for starting rate (lower limit)	Profit limit for starting rate marginal relief (upper limit)	Marginal relief fraction for starting rate
2001	30	20(1)	300,000(1)	1,500,000(1)	1/40(1)	10(1)	10,000(1)	50,000(1)	1/40(1)
2000	30	20	300,000	1,500,000	1/40	10	10,000	50,000	1/40
1999	30	20	300,000	1,500,000	1/40	–	–	–	–
1998	31	21	300,000	1,500,000	1/40	–	–	–	–
1997	31	21	300,000	1,500,000	1/40	–	–	–	–
1996	33	24	300,000	1,500,000	9/400	–	–	–	–
1995	33	25	300,000	1,500,000	1/50	–	–	–	–
1994	33	25	300,000	1,500,000	1/50	–	–	–	–

Notes

(1) The starting and small companies' rates and limits for the financial year 2001 will be set by future legislation.

(2) For marginal small companies' relief, there is an effective rate of tax in the margin, i.e. between the above lower and upper limits, which *exceeds* the full rate. For the financial years 1997 and 1998, i.e. the years to 31 March 1998 and 1999 respectively, the marginal rate is 33.5%. For the financial years 1999 and 2000, i.e. the years to 31 March 2000 and 2001 respectively, the marginal rate is 32.5%. For the financial year 2000 there is an effective marginal rate of 22.5% on profits subject to the starting rate marginal relief i.e. on profits between £10,000 and £50,000.

(3) The lower and upper limits for the small companies' rate and the small companies' marginal relief, as well as the similar lower and upper limits for the starting rate, are reduced proportionally:
- for accounting periods of less than 12 months; and
- in the case of associated companies, by dividing the limits by the total number of non-dormant associated companies.

(4) Special provisions apply to 'close investment holding companies'. In particular, they do not receive the benefit of the small companies' rate or the starting rate and so are taxable entirely at the full rate regardless of the level of their profits.

Changes to dividend treatment

The 1997 *Finance (No. 2) Act* contains changes to the treatment of dividends (and other distributions on which ACT is due) affecting companies (other than charitable companies) and pension providers with effect from 2 July 1997. For dividends paid after that date, it is no longer possible to claim a payment of the associated tax credits.

Companies continue to account for ACT at 20 per cent until 5 April 1999. The *Finance Act* 1998 abolishes the requirement for companies to account for ACT with effect for qualifying distributions paid on or after 6 April 1999. There are restrictions to tax relief for surplus unutilised ACT at that date.

Marginal relief

(ICTA 1988, s. 13)

$$\text{Deduction} = (\text{Upper Limit} - \text{Profits}) \times \frac{\text{Basic profits}}{\text{Profits}} \times \text{Marginal Relief Fraction}$$

'Profits' means profits as finally computed for corporation tax purposes *plus* franked investment income *excluding* franked investment income from companies in the same group (distributions are treated as coming from within the group if the dividends so received are group income or would be group income if the companies so elected or, for distributions made on or after 6 April 1999, if the distributions are received from a company which is a 51 per cent subsidiary or a consortium company, the recipient being a member of the consortium) *plus* foreign income dividends (up to 5 April 1999).

'Basic profits' means profits as finally computed for corporation tax purposes (also known as 'profits chargeable to corporation tax').

Similar provisions apply for calculating marginal relief for the starting rate effective from 1 April 2000.

Advance corporation tax rates

(ICTA 1988, s. 14(3))

ACT is abolished for distributions made on or after 6 April 1999 and ceases to be payable with effect from that date.

Year	ACT rate	Year	ACT rate
1998–99	1/4	1994–95	1/4
1997–98	1/4		
1996–97	1/4		
1995–96	1/4		

The rates shown apply for the relevant financial years and apply to the amount or value of the distribution, e.g. the net dividend.

Charge on loans to participators

(ICTA 1988, s. 419)

For loans or advances made before 6 April 1999, the rate of charge was equal to the rate of ACT for the financial year in which the loan or advance was made.

For loans or advances made on or after 6 April 1999, the rate of charge is determined by specific legislation. Under the provisions of *Finance Act* 1998 this is fixed at 25 per cent of the amount of the loan or advance until further notice.

Regardless of the rate applicable or the method of calculating tax due, the change itself is separate from other liabilities, being treated 'as if it were an amount of corporation tax chargeable on the company'.

Due dates

Mainstream tax

(ICTA 1988, s. 10)

Self Assessment (accounting periods ending on or after 1 July 1999)
The *Finance Act* 1998 provides for the payment of corporation tax by 'large' companies (defined in accordance with the small companies' marginal relief upper limit) in instalments. The system is to be phased in over a four-year period with 60 per cent, 72 per cent and 88 per cent of a large company's liability in the first, second and third year of the change being payable in instalments.

The balance not payable in instalments will continue to be due in accordance with the previous provisions (see 'Pay and File' below). Companies which are 'large' because of the number of associated companies or because of substantial dividend income will not have to pay by instalments if their corporation tax liabilities are less than £10,000 (for accounting periods ending after 30 June 2000; previously the limit was £5,000). Companies which become 'large' in an accounting period, having previously had profits below the upper limit, may be exempt from instalment arrangements in certain circumstances. Instalments fall due on the fourteenth day of the seventh, tenth, thirteenth and sixteenth months after the start of a 12-month accounting period. Groups containing 'large' companies will be able to pay corporation tax on a group-wide basis.

Pay and File (accounting periods ending after 30 September 1993)
Payable nine months and one day after the end of an accounting period *without* the making of an assessment.

Advance corporation tax

14 days after end of return period.

Return periods end on 31 March, 30 June, 30 September, 31 December and at end of accounting period.

In practice, if the rate of ACT changes no separate return is required in respect of the period to 5 April, treated as a notional accounting period in determining (inter alia) the company's liability for ACT.

ACT is abolished for distributions made on or after 6 April 1999; see p. 46.

Charge under ICTA 1988, s. 419 (loans to participators)

Self Assessment and Pay and File
Nine months and one day after the end of the accounting period in which the loan was advanced (the limit was 14 days for loans made in accounting periods ending after 30 September 1993 and before 31 March 1996), with no need for assessment and interest runs from the due date.

Filing deadlines

(TMA 1970, s. 11 for accounting periods ending before 1 July 1999, FA 1998, Sch. 18, para. 14 for accounting periods ending on or after 1 July 1999)

The filing date for a return of profits (CT 600, or approved substitute) is generally the latest of the three dates outlined below. Note that only the first two of these are relevant unless the company is making a return in respect of an accounting period forming part of a period of account which is greater than 12 months in length.

- 12 months from the end of the return period.
- Three months after the issue of a notice to deliver a corporation tax return.
- If a period of account is greater than 12 months in length, it will be divided into two or more accounting periods.

  If such a period of account is no longer than 18 months, the date for both accounting periods is 12 months from the end of the period of account.

  If such a period of account is greater than 18 months, the date for the first accounting period is 30 months from the start of the period of account. The date for the second and any subsequent accounting period is 12 months from the end of that accounting period.

Notes

Obligation to file return is not automatic but is imposed by notice issued by inspector.

Where a company is not sent a notice, and has not submitted a return, it must notify the Revenue of its chargeability within 12 months of end of accounting period. Failure to do so can result in a penalty.

In any case tax due for an accounting period should be paid by the due date.

An amended return under self assessment (accounting periods ending on or after 1 July 1999) may not be made later than 12 months after the filing date stipulated above.

Penalties

Infringement penalised	Maximum penalty	Provision	
		TMA 1970	FA 1998, Sch. 18
Failure to notify chargeability	100% of tax unpaid 12 months after end of accounting period	s. 10(3)	para. 2
Failure to make return[1] • up to 3 months after filing date • more than 3 months after filing date • at least 18 months but less than 24 months after the end of return period • 24 months or more after end of return period	*Fixed penalty*[2] £100 (persistent failure, £500) £200 (persistent failure, £1,000) *Tax-geared penalty*[3] 10% of tax unpaid at 18 months after end of return period 20% of tax unpaid at 18 months after end of return period	s. 94(1), (5) s. 94(6)	para. 17(2), (3) para. 18
Fraudulent or negligent submission of an incorrect return or accounts	100% of tax lost	s. 96	para. 20, 89
Failure to keep and preserve records (subject to specific exceptions)	Up to £3,000	–	para. 23
Failure to produce documents for purposes of an enquiry	£50 plus penalty for continued failure of £30 per day (£150 per day if determined by commissioners)	–	para. 29

Notes

(1) The following transitional rules apply where notice is not served until after 1 January 1994 in relation to an accounting period ending before 1 October 1993 (Revenue's *Tax Bulletin*, August 1993).

- Statutory filing date before 1 October 1994; the late filing penalty of £100 is not charged if return delivered before 1 October 1994; the late filing penalty of £200 is reduced to £100 if return filed before 1 January 1995.
- Where date on which a tax-geared late penalty incurred falls before 1 April 1995, no tax-geared penalty if return filed by that date.
- Where date on which late-filing penalty of 20% is incurred falls before 1 October 1995, penalty reduced to 10% if return filed between 1 April 1995 and 1 October 1995.

(2) Fixed penalty does not apply if return filed by date allowed by Registrar of Companies.

(3) Tax-geared penalty is charged in addition to fixed penalty. Where more than one tax-geared penalty is incurred the total penalty shall not exceed the largest individual penalty on that tax.

Interest

Interest on	Interest runs from	Provision in TMA 1970
Overdue ACT and income tax deducted from certain payments[1]	14 days after end of return period	s. 87
Overdue corporation tax	Date tax due and payable (nine months and one day after end of accounting period)[2]	s. 87A
Tax due under ICTA 1988, s. 419 (loans to participators)	14 days after end of the accounting period in which loan or advance is made	s. 87A, s. 109
Corporation tax payable in instalments (see p. 67)	Date instalment is due to be paid	s. 87A (as amended by SI 1998/3175)

Note

(1) Interest provisions cease to apply to ACT for accounting periods beginning on or after 6 April 1999 following abolition of ACT; see p. 46.

(2) Where one group company is liable to interest and another group company with the same accounting period is due a repayment of corporation tax an election may be made for the overpayment to be surrendered so as to reduce the interest liability of the first company which will be treated as having paid tax at the same time as the surrendering company (FA 1989, s. 102).

Repayment interest

(ICTA 1988, s. 826)

Repayment interest on corporation tax runs from later of:

- due and payable date (nine months and one day after end of accounting period[1]); and
- date of actual payment; except for
- overpayments of instalments of corporation tax (see p. 67), when interest runs from the first instalment date on which the excess amount would have been due and payable or, if later, the date on which that excess arises; and
- for companies outside the instalments regime, if tax was paid earlier than the normal due date, when interest on repayments in advance of agreement of liability runs from the first instalment date on which the excess amount would have been due and payable had the instalments regime applied or, the date on which the amount repayable was originally paid, whichever is later[1]

Note

[1] Interest on repayments of income tax deducted at source from income will run from the day after the end of the accounting period in which the income was received for accounting periods under self assessment.

Interest on overpaid/underpaid tax: income/expense

Under self-assessment interest on repayments to companies is taxable and interest payable by all companies on underpaid tax is allowable for corporation tax. They are treated as credits or debits respectively on non-trading loan relationships.

Time limits for elections and claims

In the absence of any provision to the contrary, the normal rule is that claims are to be made within six years from the end of the relevant chargeable period (TMA 1970, s. 43(1); FA 1998, Sch. 18, para. 46(1) for accounting periods within self-assessment).

For details of time limits relating to payment of tax, see pp. 10, 47, 80 and 94.

In certain cases the Board *may* permit an extension of the strict time limit in relation to certain elections and claims.

Provision	Time limit	Statutory reference
Stock transferred to a connected party on cessation of trade to be valued at higher of cost or sale price	2 years from end of accounting period in which trade ceased	ICTA 1988, s. 100(1C)
Carry-back of ACT (from accounting periods beginning *before* 6 April 1999 only)	2 years from end of accounting period	ICTA 1988, s. 239(3)
Surrender of ACT (from accounting periods beginning *before* 6 April 1999 only)	6 years from end of surrendering company's accounting period	ICTA 1988, s. 240(1), (6)
Carry-forward of trading losses for accounting periods ending after 30 September 1993	Relief is given automatically	ICTA 1988, s. 393(1)
Set-off of trading losses against profits of the same, or an earlier, accounting period	2 years from end of accounting period in which loss incurred	ICTA 1988, s. 393A(1), (10) and formerly s. 393(1), (11)

Provision	Time limit	Statutory reference
Group relief • where claimant company's accounting period is under self-assessment	Claims to group relief must be made (or withdrawn) by the later of: (1) 12 months after the claimant company's filing date for the return for the accounting period covered by the claim; (2) 30 days after the issue of a closure notice is issued on the completion of an enquiry; (3) 30 days after the Revenue issue a notice of amendment to a return following the completion of an enquiry (issued where the company fails to amend the return itself); or (4) 30 days after the determination of any appeal against a Revenue amendment (as in (3) above). 'Enquiry' in the above does not include a restricted enquiry into an amendment to a return (restricted because the time limit for making an enquiry into the return itself has expired), where the amendment consists of a group relief claim or withdrawal of claim. These time limits have priority over any other general time limits for amending returns and are subject to the Revenue permitting an extension to the time limits.	ICTA 1988, s. 412 and FA 1998, Sch. 18, para. 74
• where claimant company's accounting period is under Pay and File	6 years from end of claimant company's accounting period (or such longer time as the Revenue permit subject to a maximum extension of 3 months) although a claim can only be made within 2 years of the end of the accounting period where an assessment has become final	ICTA 1988, s. 412, Sch. 17A, para. 2
Set-off of loss on disposal of shares in unquoted trading company against income of investment company	2 years from end of accounting period	ICTA 1988, s. 573(2)
Surrender of company tax refund within group (for accounting periods ending after 30 September 1993)	Before refund made to surrendering company	FA 1989, s. 102(2)
Certain plant and machinery treated as 'short life' assets	2 years from end of chargeable/basis period	CAA 1990, s. 37(1), (2)

Provision	Time limit	Statutory reference
Set-off of capital allowances given by discharge or repayment[(1)]	2 years from end of accounting period	CAA 1990, s. 145(3), (5)
Transfer between connected parties of certain assets, eligible for capital allowances, at tax-written down value	2 years from date of sale (for transfers after 29 July 1988)	CAA 1990, s. 158(1)
Relief for non-trading exchange losses (accounting periods ending before 1 April 1996)	2 years from end of accounting period to which relievable amount relates	FA 1993, s. 131(3), (4), (14)
Notification of expenditure on plant and machinery on which capital allowances to be claimed[(2)]	2 years from end of accounting period into which claim relates	FA 1994, s. 118(3)
Relief for a non-trading deficit on loan relationships (including any non-trading exchange losses arising in accounting periods ending after 31 March 1996)	2 years from end of period in which deficit arises, or, in the case of a claim to carry forward the deficit, 2 years from end of the accounting period following the deficit period, or within such further period as the Board may allow	FA 1996, s. 83(6), (7) (and as applied to exchange losses by FA 1993, s. 130(2))

Provision	Time limit	Statutory reference
General claim to capital allowances under self-assessment	Claims to capital allowances must be made (or amended or withdrawn) by the later of: (1) 12 months after the claimant company's filing date for the return for the accounting period covered by the claim; (2) 30 days after the issue of a closure notice is issued on the completion of an enquiry; (3) 30 days after the Revenue issue a notice of amendment to a return following the completion of an enquiry (issued where the company fails to amend the return itself); or (4) 30 days after the determination of any appeal against a Revenue amendment (as in (3) above). 'Enquiry' in the above does not include a restricted enquiry into an amendment to a return (restricted because the time limit for making an enquiry into the return itself has expired), where the amendment consists of a capital allowances claim, amendment or withdrawal of a claim. These time limits have priority over any other general time limits for amending returns and are subject to the Revenue permitting an extension to the time limits.	FA 1998, Sch. 18, para. 82

Notes

(1) Allowances previously given by discharge or repayment of tax on assets used for letting have been given instead in arriving at the profits of a Sch. A business, with effect from the following dates:

- 6 April 1995 generally for the purposes of income tax;
- 1 April 1997 (accounting periods ending on or after) for plant and machinery for the purposes of corporation tax; and
- 1 April 1998 (accounting periods ending on or after) for all other assets for the purposes of corporation tax.

(2) Requirement to notify abolished by Finance Act 2000 with effect for claims where the time limit falls after 31 March 2000.

GENERAL

Capital allowances: rates

Machinery and plant (CAA 1990, s. 22)

	First year allowances[4] (FYAs)			Writing down allowances[4]	
Date expenditure incurred	Small businesses[1][2]	Larger businesses	Long-life assets[5]	All businesses	Long-life assets[5]
On or after 1 April 2000	40%[6]/100%[3]	Nil	Nil	25%	6%
2 July 1998–31 March 2000	40%[6]	Nil	Nil	25%	6%
2 July 1997–1 July 1998	50%	Nil	12%	25%	6%
26 November 1996–1 July 1997	Nil	Nil	Nil	25%	6%
1 November 1993–1 November 1996	Nil			25%	
1 November 1992–31 October 1993	40%			25%	

Notes

[1] A 'small business' is defined using the *Companies Act* 1985, s. 247, 249 definitions for small and medium sized companies. Essentially to qualify a business must meet any two of three criteria: (i) Turnover under £11.2m p.a.; (ii) balance sheet total under £5.6m; (iii) no more than 250 employees. If a company is a member of a group both the company and the group must meet the criteria (CAA 1990, s. 22A).

[2] Expenditure incurred by a small business between 12 May 1998 and 11 May 2002 on machinery and plant for use primarily in Northern Ireland qualifies for a FYA of 100%. This regionally based relief does *not* apply to long life assets, aircraft, hovercraft, certain goods vehicles and certain expenditure on assets used in agriculture, fishing or fish farming that is unapproved by the Dept. of Agriculture for Northern Ireland (CAA 1990, s. 22(3CA)ff.).

[3] 100% FYAs are to be temporarily available for expenditure by small businesses on information technology equipment (computers, software and internet-enabled mobile telephones) in the period from 1 April 2000 to 31 March 2003 (FA 2000).

[4] FYAs are *not* available for expenditure on cars, ships, railway assets, machinery and plant for leasing, and (except for the 12% rate) long life assets. The amount of a FYA claim may be reduced to any specified amount (CAA 1990, s. 22(7)).

[5] Long life assets have an expected useful economic life of at least 25 years when new. Only businesses expending more than £100,000 in a year on such assets are within these special rules. Cars, certain non-recreational sea-going ships, railway assets and fixtures in buildings used as dwelling houses, retail shops, showrooms, hotels or offices cannot be long life assets. (CAA 1990, s. 38A-38H).

[6] 40% FYAs were introduced for a 12-month period by FA 1998; the duration of the relief was extended by FA 1999 and it is to be made permanent by FA 2000.

[7] Where expenditure exceeding £12,000 is incurred on a motor car (after 10 March 1992) the maximum Writing Down Allowance available is restricted to £3,000 per annum.

Industrial Buildings;[1] Hotels;[2] and Agricultural buildings and structures[3]

Date expenditure incurred	Initial allowance[4]	Writing down allowance
On or after 1 November 1993	Nil	4%
1 November 1992–31 October 1993	20%	4%
1 April 1986–31 October 1992	Nil	4%

Notes

[1] The non-industrial element of an industrial building will qualify for allowances provided it does not exceed 25%. Dwelling-houses, retail shops and showrooms, offices and hotels are not 'industrial buildings' (CAA 1990, s. 18). Prior to 1986 high rates of initial allowances (75% and 100%) applied in some years, for some buildings.

[2] A qualifying hotel must provide standard hotel facilities; have at least 10 letting bedrooms and be open for at least four months between April-October, inclusive (CAA 1990, s. 19).

[3] Includes expenditure on farmhouses and buildings, cottages, fences and other works incurred for the purposes of husbandry on agricultural land (a maximum of 1/3 of expenditure on farmhouses may qualify) (CAA 1990, s. 123, 124).

Enterprise Zones:[1] Industrial Buildings; Hotels and Commercial Buildings or structures[2]

Date expenditure incurred	Initial allowance[3]	Writing down allowance
Contract to be made within 10 years of site being included within the enterprise zone (but not expenditure incurred over 20 years after the date of the site being included)	100%	25%

Notes
[1] Areas designated by Orders made under the *Local Government, Planning and Land Act* 1980 or equivalent Northern Ireland legislation (CAA 1990, s. 21(4)).
[2] Buildings or structures used for the purposes of a trade, profession or vocation (but not an industrial building or qualifying hotel) or used as offices; but not a dwelling house (CAA 1990, s. 21(5)).
[3] The claim to initial allowance may be reduced to any specified amount (CAA 1990, s. 1(5)).

Dredging (CAA 1990, s. 134)

Date expenditure incurred	Initial allowance	Writing down allowance
On or after 1 April 1986	Nil	4%

Mineral extraction[1] (CAA 1990, s. 98)

Date expenditure incurred	Initial allowance	Writing down allowance
On or after 1 April 1986	Nil	25%[2]

Notes
[1] Includes mines, oil wells and geothermal energy sources.
[2] Certain expenditure, on the acquisition of a mineral deposit and/or rights over such a deposit, qualifies for a 10% WDA.

Scientific research[1] (CAA 1990, s. 98)

Date expenditure incurred	Initial allowance	Writing down allowance
On or after 5 November 1962	100%	No provision for WDAs

Notes
[1] Covers expenditure incurred on any activities in the fields of natural or applied science for the extension of knowledge, but not that incurred on the acquisition of rights in, or arising out of, scientific research.

Patent rights[1] and Know-how[2] (ICTA 1988, s. 520, 530)

Date expenditure incurred	Initial allowance	Writing down allowance
On or after 1 April 1986	Nil	25%

Notes
[1] The purchase of patent rights includes the acquisition of a licence in respect of a patent.
[2] 'Know-how' means any industrial information and techniques likely to assist in: (i) the manufacture or processing of goods or materials; (ii) all aspects of working a mine, oil well or mineral deposit; (iii) carrying out agricultural, forestry or fishing operations. The Revenue consider that know-how not directly related to manufacturing or processing operations is 'commercial' know-how and cannot qualify for these allowances (IRInt. 46; *Tax Bulletin*; August 1993, p. 86).

Dwelling houses let under assured tenancies (CAA 1990, s. 84)

Date expenditure incurred	Initial allowance	Writing down allowance
1 April 1986–31 March 1992	Nil	4%

Enterprise zones

Enterprise zones have been designated as follows:

Statutory instrument	Area	Start date
1981/309	Belfast	21 October 1981
1981/757	Lower Swansea Valley	11 June 1981
1981/764	Corby	22 June 1981
1981/852	Dudley	10 July 1981
1981/950	Wakefield (Langthwaite Grange)	31 July 1981
1981/975	Clydebank	3 August 1981
1981/1024	Salford	12 August 1981
1981/1025	Trafford Park	12 August 1981
1981/1069	Glasgow	18 August 1981
1981/1070	Gateshead	25 August 1981
1981/1071	Newcastle	25 August 1981
1981/1072	Speke	25 August 1981
1981/1378	Hartlepool	23 October 1981
1982/462	Isle of Dogs	26 April 1982
1983/226	Londonderry	13 September 1983
1983/896	Delyn and Flint	21 July 1983
1983/907	Wellingborough	26 July 1983
1983/1007	Rotherham	16 August 1983
1983/1304	Scunthorpe (excluding Glanford)	23 September 1983
1983/1305	Wakefield (extended to Dale Lane and Kinsley)	23 September 1983
1983/1331	Workington (Allerdale)	4 October 1983
1983/1359	Invergordon	7 October 1983
1983/1452	North-West Kent (Gillingham and Gravesend)	31 October 1983
1983/1473	Middlesbrough (Britannia)	8 November 1983
1983/1639	North-East Lancashire (Burnley, Hyndburn, Pendle and Rossendale)	7 December 1983
1983/1816	Arbroath	9 January 1984
1983/1817	Dundee	9 January 1984
1983/1852	Telford	13 January 1984
1984/347	Glanford (Flixborough)	13 April 1984
1984/443–444	Milford Haven Waterway	24 April 1984
1984/1403	Dudley (extended to Round Oak)	3 October 1984
1985/137	Lower Swansea Valley (extended)	6 March 1985
1986/1557	North-West Kent (extended to Chatham and Rochester-upon-Medway)	10 October 1986
1989/145	Inverclyde	3 March 1989
1989/794	Sunderland (Castletown and Doxford Park)	27 April 1990
1989/795	Sunderland (Hylton Riverside and Southwick)	27 April 1990
1993/23	Lanarkshire (Hamilton)	1 February 1993
1993/24	Lanarkshire (Motherwell)	1 February 1993
1993/25	Lanarkshire (Monklands)	1 February 1993
1995/2624	Dearne Valley (Barnsley, Doncaster, Rotherham)	3 November 1995
1995/2625	Holmewood (North East Derbyshire)	3 November 1995
1995/2738	Bassetlaw	16 November 1995
1995/2758	Ashfield	21 November 1995
1995/2812	East Durham (No. 1 to No. 6)	29 November 1995
1996/106	Tyne Riverside (North Tyneside)	19 February 1996
1996/1981	Tyne Riverside (Silverlink North Scheme)	26 August 1996
1996/1981	Tyne Riverside (Silverlink Business Park Scheme)	26 August 1996
1996/1981	Tyne Riverside (Middle Engine Lane Scheme)	26 August 1996
1996/1981	Tyne Riverside (New York Industrial Park Scheme)	26 August 1996
1996/1981	Tyne Riverside (Balliol Business Park West Scheme)	26 August 1996
1996/1981	Tyne Riverside (Balliol Business Park East Scheme)	26 August 1996
1996/2435	Tyne Riverside (Baltic Enterprise Park Scheme)	21 October 1996
1996/2435	Tyne Riverside (Viking Industrial Park – Wagonway West Scheme)	21 October 1996
1996/2435	Tyne Riverside (Viking Industrial Park – Blackett Street Scheme)	21 October 1996
1996/2435	Tyne Riverside (Viking Industrial Park – Western Road Scheme)	21 October 1996

Note
Enterprise zones last for ten years from the start date (CAA 1990, s. 6(1)).

Lease premiums

Amount of premium assessable under Sch. A when lease granted, where duration of lease is at least one year but not more than 50 years (ICTA 1988, s. 34):

$$P \times \frac{51 - D}{50}$$

where P = total premium; and
D = duration of lease in complete years (ignoring any additional part of a year).

Amount taken into account in calculating a chargeable gain will be the balance of the premium (TCGA 1992, s. 240 and Sch. 8, para. 5, 7) for which the restriction of allowable expenditure is applicable:

Length of lease in years	Amount chargeable as gains %	Amount within Sch. A %
Over 50	100	0
50	98	2
49	96	4
48	94	6
47	92	8
46	90	10
45	88	12
44	86	14
43	84	16
42	82	18
41	80	20
40	78	22
39	76	24
38	74	26
37	72	28
36	70	30
35	68	32
34	66	34
33	64	36
32	62	38
31	60	40
30	58	42
29	56	44
28	54	46
27	52	48
26	50	50

Length of lease in years	Amount chargeable as gains %	Amount within Sch. A %
25	48	52
24	46	54
23	44	56
22	42	58
21	40	60
20	38	62
19	36	64
18	34	66
17	32	68
16	30	70
15	28	72
14	26	74
13	24	76
12	22	78
11	20	80
10	18	82
9	16	84
8	14	86
7	12	88
6	10	90
5	8	92
4	6	94
3	4	96
2	2	98
1 or less	0	100

Amount of lease premium allowed as a Sch. D, Case I or II deduction:

$$\frac{\text{Schedule A charge on landlord}}{\text{D (as above)}} \times \frac{\text{Days in accounting or basis period}}{365}$$

Lease rentals for expensive motor cars

In respect of contracts entered into after 10 March 1992, the restricted deduction for hire charges of motor cars if the retail price was greater than £12,000 is as follows (CAA 1990, s. 35(2)):

$$\text{Allowable amount} = \frac{£12{,}000 + \tfrac{1}{2}(\text{retail price} - £12{,}000)}{\text{retail price}} \times \text{hire charge}$$

For contracts entered into prior to 11 March 1992, the restriction applies if the retail price was greater than £8,000. The restricted deduction is as follows:

$$\text{Allowable amount} = \frac{£8{,}000 + \tfrac{1}{2}(\text{retail price} - £8{,}000)}{\text{retail price}} \times \text{hire charge}$$

Charitable Giving

Gift Aid (FA 1990, s. 25; ICTA 1988, s. 339)

Donations of cash by individuals and close companies to charities, etc.	Minimum qualifying cash donation[(1)] (net of basic rate income tax)
On or after 6 April 2000	No minimum donation
16 March 1993–5 April 2000	£250
7 May 1992–15 March 1993	£400

Note

[(1)] There has never been a minimum qualifying donation for non-close companies.

Millennium Gift Aid (FA 1998, s. 48)

Gifts by individuals to relieve poverty and advance education in designated countries[(1)]	Minimum qualifying cash donation (net of basic rate income tax)
31 July 1998 to 31 December 2000	£100[(2)]

Notes

[(1)] Countries are designated by Treasury Orders and include those in Appendix 5 to the World Bank's 1997 Annual report (as revised from time to time) as eligible for certain funding (and Kosovo, for gifts made after 5 April 1999).

[(2)] The minimum donation may be made by a single payment or by aggregated instalments. No such installment may either exceed £250, or be the second or subsequent one to exceed £100.

Gifts of assets

Nature of asset	Date(s) of relief	Effect of relief
Plant or machinery used by, or stock manufactured or sold by a trader that is given to a charity, etc. (ICTA 1988, s. 83A)	From 27 July 1999	No disposal value brought into account as trading receipt or for capital allowances purposes
Plant or machinery used by, or stock manufactured or sold by, a trader that is given to a charity for medical or educational purposes for use in specific, designated countries (FA 1998, s. 47)[1]	21 August 1998 to 26 July 1999	No disposal value brought into account as trading receipt or for capital allowances purposes
Listed shares and securities, unlisted shares and securities that are dealt in on recognised stock exchanges, units in unit trusts, etc. given to a charity by an individual or company (FA 2000)	From April 2000	The full value of the gift is deductible when computing profits for IT or CT purposes.
Property settled by gift on a UK resident trust which has a charity as beneficiary *and* the settlor retains an interest (FA 2000)	From April 2000	The trust income allocated to the settlor under ICTA 1988, Pt. XV wil be reduced by an amount equal to the income paid to the charity in the year

Notes

[1] Countries are designated by Treasury Order and include those in Appendix 5 to the World Bank's 1997 Annual report (as revised from time to time) as eligible for certain funding. FA 1998, s. 47 was repealed by FA 1999, s. 55 which introduced relief under ICTA 1988, s. 83A.

Certificates of tax deposit (CTDs)

The interest rates that follow apply to CTDs issued under the Series 7 prospectus. No further deposits were accepted under the Series 6 prospectus after 30 September 1993.

CTDs (Series 7) can be purchased to settle most tax liabilities, except PAYE, VAT and corporation tax falling due under Pay and File, or for subsequent encashment. (No CTDs are available for purchase for use against corporation tax liabilities since the start of the Pay and File regime.) A higher rate of interest is paid if the CTD is used in payment of tax. Interest is allowed/paid gross and is taxable.

Series 7 rates of interest vary according to the period for which the deposit is held. The rates in force at issue apply for one year; thereafter the rate applicable is that on the most recent anniversary of the date of issue.

Deposits must be maintained at £2,000 or over. A deposit of less than £100,000 can be made at any tax collection office. Larger deposits must be sent to the Bank of England (Drawing Office) (for the General Account of the Commissioners of Inland Revenue, No. 23411007) with a confirmatory letter to the Central Accounting Office (CTD), Inland Revenue (A), Barrington Road, Worthing, West Sussex, BN12 4XH.

Copies of the Series 7 prospectus, giving full details concerning CTDs, can be obtained from any collection office or the Central Accounting Office.

Rates applicable over recent years have been as follows:

Certificates of tax deposit (Series 7): rates of interest

Deposits on or after	Deposits under £100,000		Deposits of £100,000 or more: Deposits held for under 1 month		Deposits held for 1 to under 3 months		Deposits held for 3 to under 6 months		Deposits held for 6 to under 9 months		Deposits held for 9–12 months	
	Applied in payment of tax %	Cash value %	Applied in payment of tax %	Cash value %	Applied in payment of tax %	Cash value %	Applied in payment of tax %	Cash value %	Applied in payment of tax %	Cash value %	Applied in payment of tax %	Cash value %
1 Oct. 1993	2¾	1¼	2¾	1¼	5¼	2½	5	2½	4¾	2¼	4½	2¼
24 Nov. 1993	1¾	1	1¾	1	4¼	2¼	4	2	3¾	2	3¾	1¾
9 Feb. 1994	1½	¾	1½	¾	4	2	3¾	1¾	3½	1¾	3½	1¾
13 Sept. 1994	2	1	2	1	4¾	2½	4¾	2½	5	2½	5½	2¾
8 Dec. 1994	2½	1¼	2½	1¼	5¼	2¾	5½	2¾	5¾	3	6	3
3 Feb. 1995	3	1½	3	1½	5¾	3	5¾	3	6	3	6¼	3¼
14 Dec. 1995	2½	1¼	2½	1¼	5½	2¾	5	2½	5	2½	4¾	2½
19 Jan. 1996	2¾	1½	2¾	1½	5¼	2¾	4¾	2½	4¾	2½	4½	2¼
11 Mar. 1996	2½	1¼	2½	1¼	5	2½	4¾	2½	4¾	2½	4¼	2¼
7 June 1996	2¼	1¼	2¼	1½	4¾	2½	4¾	2½	4¾	2½	4¾	2½
31 Oct. 1996	2½	1¼	2½	1¼	5¼	2¾	5	2½	5	2½	5	2½
7 May 1997	2¾	1½	2¾	1½	5½	2¾	5¼	2¾	5½	2¾	5¼	2¾
9 June 1997	3	1½	3	1½	5½	2¾	5½	2¾	5½	2¾	5½	2¾
11 July 1997	3¼	1¾	3¼	1¾	6	3	5¾	3	5¾	3	6	3
8 Aug. 1997	4½	2¼	4½	2¼	6	3	6	3	6	3	5¾	3
7 Nov. 1997	4	2	4	2	6½	3¼	6½	3¼	6¼	3¼	6¼	3¼
5 June 1998	4	2	4	2	6½	3¼	6¼	3¼	6¼	3¼	6	3
9 Oct. 1998	3¾	2	3¾	2	6¼	3¼	5¾	3	5½	2¾	5¼	2¾
6 Nov. 1998	3¼	1¾	3¼	1¾	5¾	3	5¼	2¾	5	2½	4¾	2½
5 Feb. 1999	1¾	1	1¾	1	4½	2¼	4	2	3¾	2	3¾	2
9 Apr. 1999	1¾	1	1¾	1	4½	2	4	2	3¾	2	3¾	2
11 June 1999	1½	¾	1½	¾	4	2	4	2	4	2	4	2
9 Sept. 1999	1¾	1	1¾	1	4½	2¼	4½	2¼	4½	2¼	4½	2¼
4 Nov. 1999	2	1	2	1	5	2½	4¾	2½	4¾	2½	4¾	2½
14 Jan. 2000	2¼	1¼	2¼	1¼	5	2½	5	2½	5	2½	5¼	2¾
11 Feb. 2000	2½	1¼	2½	1¼	5¼	2¾	5	2½	5¼	2¾	5¼	2¾

Interest and surcharges 2000–2001

Payment of tax, etc. normal due dates

Income tax, see p. 10.
Corporation tax, see p. 47.
Capital gains tax, see p. 80.
Inheritance tax, see p. 94.

Income tax and capital gains tax

Interest (TMA 1970, s. 86)

Interest is payable from the 'relevant date' (see the rules as regards payment of tax at p. 10):

Payment	Relevant date
First interim payment[(1)]	31 January 2001
Second interim payment	31 July 2001
Final payment	31 January 2002
Tax due on an amendment to a return	31 January 2002
Tax due on determination of appeal	31 January 2002

Note

Where notice to make a return is issued after 31 October 2000, then, provided there has been no failure to notify chargeability under TMA 1970, s. 7, the relevant date becomes the last day in the period of three months beginning with the day notice to make a return was given.

(1) Where the taxpayer has provided the Revenue in good time with the information required to issue a statement of account ahead of the payment date of 31 January, but no statement is received before 1 January, interest on the tax to be paid will run from 30 days after the taxpayer is actually notified rather than from 31 January.

Loss due to taxpayer's fault (TMA 1970, s. 88 – repealed by FA 1996)

The distinction between 'default' interest (TMA 1970, s. 88) and simple 'delay' interest (TMA 1970, s. 86) does not apply for 1996–97 onwards (1997–98 for partnerships in business since before 6 April 1994), nor to assessments for 1995–96 and earlier years made after 5 April 1998.

Surcharges (TMA 1970, s. 59C)

Surcharges arise as follows:

Tax overdue	Surcharge
28 days	5% of tax overdue
6 months	further 5% of tax overdue

Note

Tax is not subject to a surcharge if it is taken into account for penalties for failure to notify – return over 12 months late or incorrect return (see p. 6). A surcharge will be repaid if one of these penalties is subsequently levied.

Surcharges apply to:

- final tax payments on self-assessments (this includes any amounts due as interim payments which remain unpaid);
- tax on inspector's amendments to a self-assessment made during or as a result of an audit;
- discovery assessments; and
- late payments of tax on assessments for 1995–96 and earlier years, where the assessment was made after 5 April 1998.

Surcharges are payable 30 days after the inspector's notice imposing the surcharge and interest is charged on surcharges not paid when due.

Corporation tax and advance corporation tax

(TMA 1970, s. 87, 87A)

Interest runs from the date tax becomes due, as follows:

Tax	Assessment not appealed or no postponement application	Assessment appealed with postponement application: Tax not postponed but charged by assessment	Assessment appealed with postponement application: Tax not originally charged but due or tax postponed but payable
Corp. tax	**Under Pay and File and Corporation Tax Self Assessment** In respect of accounting periods ending after 30 September 1993 corporation tax is payable 9 months and one day after the end of an accounting period *without* the making of an assessment		
	Accounting periods ending before 1 October 1993		
	Later of 9 months and one day after end of accounting period or 30 days after assessment date	Later of 9 months and one day after end of accounting period or 30 days from postponement determination	Later of 9 months and one day after end of accounting period or 30 days after determination of appeal; or if (i) later than 15 months after end of accounting period; (ii) later of 15 months after end of accounting period or 30 days after original assessment
ACT[1][2]	14 days after end of return period		

Note

[1] Also income tax deducted at source on company payments.

[2] ACT abolished in respect of qualifying distributions made after 5 April 1999.

PAYE

From 19 April 1993 in relation to 1992–93 and subsequent years of assessment interest runs on overdue tax from the fourteenth day after the end of the tax year to which the tax relates. The interest rate is the general rate for overdue tax as varied from time to time (see p. 65).

Value added tax

For prescribed accounting periods beginning after 31 March 1990 interest may be due (VATA 1994, s. 74; see p. 113). The reckonable dates are:

- *interest on overdue tax*: due date for submission of return (usually last day of month following end of return period);
- *interest on tax incorrectly repaid*: seven days after issue of instruction directing payment of amount incorrectly repaid.

Assessments of interest made after 30 September 1993 are restricted to the last three years (VATA 1994, s. 74(3)).

From 7 September 1994, Customs normally do not assess interest if it does not represent 'commercial restitution'.

From 1 February 1995, Customs normally do not assess interest on voluntary disclosures notified to Customs when the net underdeclaration is £2,000 or less. Customs' policy was already not to assess interest where a current-period adjustment is made.

From 6 July 1998 interest rates are varied (usually from the sixth day of a month) in accordance with a formula based on the average base lending rates of the main clearing banks (*Air Passenger Duty and Other Indirect Taxes (Interest Rate) Regulations* 1998 (SI 1998/1461)).

National Insurance contributions

Social Security Contributions and Benefits Act 1992, s. 1(4) and Sch. 1, para. 6 contains provisions enabling interest to be charged on Class 1 and Class 1A contributions.

From 19 April 1993 interest is charged on Class 1 contributions unpaid after the fourteenth day after the end of the tax year in which they were due. Interest is due on Class 1A contributions unpaid 14 days after the end of the tax year in which they were due to be paid. Interest on overdue Class 4 contributions is payable in relation to 1992–93 and subsequent years of assessment (*Social Security Contributions and Benefits Act* 1992, Sch. 2, para. 6).

Rates of interest on overdue tax

The following table gives the rates of interest applicable under FA 1989, s. 178 and prescribed rates of interest (VATA 1994, s. 74 and former TMA 1970, s. 89). The rates apply to interest charged on overdue tax, with the exception of inheritance tax. From 6 February 1997 the rate for corporation tax diverges, see p. 67.

Period of application		Rate %
From 6 February 2000		8.5
6 March 1999 to	5 February 2000	7.5
6 January 1999 to	5 March 1999	8.5
6 August 1997 to	5 January 1999	9.5
6 February 1997 to	5 August 1997	8.5
6 February 1996 to	5 February 1997	6.25
6 March 1995 to	5 February 1996	7
6 October 1994 to	5 March 1995	6.25
6 January 1994 to	5 October 1994	5.5
6 March 1993 to	5 January 1994	6.25

Interest factor tables

Interest on overdue tax

The table below gives interest factors for the 1st of each month, in respect of interest on overdue tax payable under TMA 1970, s. 86, 87, 87A and 88. To find the interest accruing on a principal sum between two dates, multiply the principal sum by the difference between the factors for the dates in question. For example, interest accruing on £10,000 from 1 June 1993 to 1 February 1998 is calculated as follows: £10,000 × (3.3803 − 3.0598) = £3,205

	Jan.	Feb.	Mar.	Apr.	May	Jun.	Jul.	Aug.	Sept.	Oct.	Nov.	Dec.
1993	3.0326	3.0384	3.0442	3.0494	3.0546	3.0598	3.0650	3.0702	3.0755	3.0807	3.0859	3.0911
1994	3.0963	3.1009	3.1055	3.1101	3.1147	3.1193	3.1238	3.1284	3.1330	3.1376	3.1428	3.1480
1995	3.1532	3.1584	3.1636	3.1694	3.1753	3.1811	3.1869	3.1928	3.1986	3.2044	3.2103	3.2161
1996	3.2219	3.2278	3.2330	3.2382	3.2434	3.2486	3.2538	3.2591	3.2643	3.2695	3.2747	3.2799
1997	3.2851	3.2903	3.2974	3.3045	3.3116	3.3186	3.3257	3.3328	3.3407	3.3486	3.3565	3.3644
1998	3.3723	3.3803	3.3882	3.3961	3.4040	3.4119	3.4198	3.4278	3.4357	3.4436	3.4515	3.4594
1999	3.4673	3.4744	3.4815	3.4886	3.4957	3.5028	3.5098	3.5169	3.5240	3.5311	3.5382	3.5453
2000	3.5523	3.5594	3.5665	3.5736	3.5807	3.5878	3.5948	3.6019	3.6090	3.6161	3.6232	3.6303
2001	3.6373											

Notes

The table incorporates the interest rate change to 7.5% p.a. which came into operation on 6 March 1999 and which produces a monthly increment to the factor of 0.0071.

Where a demand for Schedule E income tax is made or other relevant tax is assessed after 18 April 1993, there is no de minimis limit for interest charged under TMA 1970, s. 86. Prior to 19 April 1993 no charge was made where the interest incurred did not exceed £30.

Where corporation tax is assessed for an accounting period beginning after 18 April 1993 there is no de minimis limit for interest charged under TMA 1970, s. 87. Prior to 19 April 1993 no charge was made where the interest incurred did not exceed £30.

trt trt97b Mp 65—trt 80

Rates of interest on tax repayments

Interest on tax repayments qualifying for repayment supplement made after 31 July 1975, except for repayments made under the Pay and File regime, is given at the following rates.

Date		Rate %
From 6 February	2000	4
From 6 March	1999 to 5 February 2000	3
From 6 January	1999 to 5 March 1999	4
From 6 August	1997 to 5 January 1999	4.75
From 6 February	1997 to 5 August 1997	4
From 6 February	1996 to 5 February 1997	6.25
From 6 March	1995 to 5 February 1996	7
From 6 October	1994 to 5 March 1995	6.25
From 6 January	1994 to 5 October 1994	5.5
From 6 March	1993 to 5 January 1994	6.25

Notes

The qualifying period is as set out below:

For individuals:

From the date of payment (deemed to be 31 January following the tax year in respect of tax deducted at source) to the date on which the order for the repayment is issued.

For periods prior to self-assessment, the qualifying period was:

Later of:

(i) due date; or

(ii) actual date of payment,

until the end of the tax month in which the repayment order is issued.

The 1997 Finance Act contained provision for interest on repayments of overpaid tax to run from the date on which tax is paid – even if this is earlier than the due date.

For companies:

Later of:

(i) 12 months after the 'material date'; or

(ii) anniversary of the 'material date' occurring next after tax paid,

until the end of the tax month in which the repayment order is issued.

The 'material date' is the earliest due date for payment of corporation tax for the relevant accounting period.

There are no de minimis limits in relation to repayments made after 5 April 1993. Previously, the minimum repayment qualifying for the supplement was £25 for individuals, £100 for companies.

Repayment supplement factor table

(ICTA 1988, s. 824ff.)

The repayment supplement on tax overpaid was introduced in 1975. Until 5 February 1997, the relevant interest factors were identical to those applying in the case of interest on tax recovered under TMA 1970, s. 88. Accordingly for months up to and including February 1997, the interest factors appearing on p. 65 may be used also in calculating repayment supplement. It must be noted, however, that in the case of repayment supplement the tax month to which the interest factor applies ends on the fifth of that month and not on the first, as with TMA 1970, s. 88. The following interest factors should be used for March 1997 onwards:

	5 Jan.	5 Feb.	5 Mar.	5 Apr.	5 May	5 Jun.	5 Jul.	5 Aug.	5 Sept.	5 Oct.	5 Nov.	5 Dec.
1997	3.2851	3.2903	3.2937	3.2970	3.3003	3.3037	3.3070	3.3103	3.3143	3.3182	3.3222	3.3261
1998	3.3301	3.3340	3.3380	3.3419	3.3459	3.3498	3.3538	3.3578	3.3618	3.3657	3.3697	3.3736
1999	3.3776	3.3809	3.3842	3.3876	3.3909	3.3942	3.3976	3.4009	3.4042	3.4076	3.4109	3.4142
2000	3.4176	3.4209	3.4242	3.4276	3.4309	3.4342	3.4376	3.4409	3.4442	3.4476	3.4509	3.4542
2001	3.4576											

Repayment interest for corporation tax

Interest on unpaid/late paid corporation tax

With effect for **interest** periods commencing on 6 February 1997, the rates of interest for the purposes of late paid or unpaid corporation tax are different from those for other taxes. From that date, the rate of interest on late paid or underpaid corporation tax will depend on the accounting period for which the tax is due and, under self assessment, the nature of the tax due:

Self assessment
For accounting periods within the self assessment regime (or CTSA – APs ending on or after 1 July 1999), these rates are distinct from those for periods before the start of self assessment because the interest is an allowable deduction for tax purposes (see below).

In addition, there are separate provisions for:

- overpaid instalments of corporation tax (which benefit from a more favourable rate – for details of payment by instalments, see below); and
- other liabilities such as the final liability due on the date specified in accordance with the table below.

Pre-self assessment
For accounting periods before the start of self assessment, there are two rates of interest applicable to all unpaid/late paid tax depending on whether the accounting period is within the Pay and File regime (APs ending after 30 September 1993) or not (i.e. periods ending before 1 October 1993).

CTSA (APs ending on or after 1-7-99)

1. Unpaid CT (other than underpaid instalments)

Period of application	Rate %
From 6 February 2000	8.5
From 6 March 1999 to 5 February 2000	7.5
From 6 January 1999 to 5 March 1999	8.5

2. Underpaid instalments

Period of application	Rate %
From 20 April 2000	7
From 21 February 2000 to 19 April 2000	8
From 21 January 2000 to 20 February 2000	7.75
From 15 November 1999 to 23 January 2000	7.50
From 20 September 1999 to 14 November 1999	7.25
From 21 June 1999 to 19 September 1999	7
From 19 April 1999 to 20 June 1999	7.25
From 15 February 1999 to 18 April 1999	7.5
From 18 January 1999 to 14 February 1999	8
Before 18 January 1999	8.25

Pre-CTSA

Period of application	Rate % pre-Pay and File	Rate % post-Pay and File
From 6 February 2000	6.5	6.75
From 6 March 1999 to 5 February 2000	5.75	5.75
From 6 January 1999 to 5 March 1999	6.5	6.5
From 6 August 1997 to 5 January 1999	7.25	7.5
From 6 February 1997 to 5 August 1997	6.25	6.25
Before 6 February 1997	(See main table)	

Interest on overpaid corporation tax

With effect for **interest** periods commencing on 6 February 1997, the rates of interest for the purposes of overpaid corporation tax are different from those for other taxes. The rate of interest on overpaid corporation tax will depend on the accounting period for which the tax is due and, under self assessment, the nature of the tax repayable:

Self assessment

For accounting periods within the self assessment regime (CTSA) i.e. APs on or after 1 July 1999, the rates of interest on repayments of overpaid corporation tax are distinct from those for pre-CTSA periods, because the interest is taxable (see below).

In addition, there are separate provisions for:

- overpaid instalments of corporation tax; and
- repayments of corporation tax made after the normal due date.

Pay and File and earlier periods

For accounting periods within Pay and File (APs ending after 30 September 1993) and accounting periods before Pay and File, interest on overpaid corporation tax, repayments of income tax and payments of tax credits in respect of franked investment income received is given at the appropriate rate shown in the relevant table below.

CTSA (APs ending on or after 1-7-99)

1. Overpaid CT (other than overpaid instalments and early payments of CT not due by instalments)

Period of application	Rate %
From 6 February 2000	5
From 6 March 1999 to 5 February 2000	4
From 6 January 1999 to 5 March 1999	5

2. Overpaid instalments and early payments of CT not due by instalments

Period of application	Rate %
From 21 February 2000	5.75
From 24 January 2000 to 20 February 2000	5.5
From 15 November 1999 to 23 January 2000	5.25
From 20 September 1999 to 14 November 1999	5
From 21 June 1999 to 19 September 1999	4.75
From 19 April 1999 to 20 June 1999	5
From 15 February 1999 to 18 April 1999	5.25
From 18 January 1999 to 14 February 1999	5.75
Before 18 January 1999	6

Pay and File

Period of application	Rate %
From 6 February 2000	3.5
From 6 March 1999 to 5 February 2000	2.75
From 6 January 1999 to 5 March 1999	3.25
From 6 August 1997 to 5 January 1999	4
From 6 February 1996 to 5 August 1997	3.25
From 6 March 1995 to 5 February 1996	4
From 6 October 1994 to 5 March 1995	3.25
From 6 January 1994 to 5 October 1994	2.5
From 1 October 1993 to 5 January 1994	3.25

Pre-Pay and File

Period of application	Rate %
From 6 February 2000	6.5
From 6 March 1999 to 5 February 2000	5.75
From 6 January 1999 to 5 March 1999	6.5
From 6 August 1997 to 5 January 1999	7.25
From 6 February 1996 to 5 August 1997	6.25
Before 6 February 1996	(See main table)

Remission of tax for official error

(ESC A19)

In some circumstances, arrears of income tax and capital gains tax are wholly or partly waived if they have arisen through failure of the Revenue to make proper and timely use of information supplied by the taxpayer so that he might reasonably believe that his affairs are in order. Concession A19 was revised with effect from 26 April 1994 to include the supply of information by the DSS which affects a taxpayer's entitlement to a retirement or widow's pension. The concession normally applies if a taxpayer is notified of the arrears more than 12 months after the end of the tax year in which the Revenue obtained the information indicating that more tax was due. It was last revised on 11 March 1996, when the scale relating the proportion of tax arrears which could be written off to the taxpayer's income was abolished.

trt trt97b Mp 69—trt 80

Fraction of arrears remitted	From 17 February 1993 to 11 March 1996 Gross income £
All	15,500 or less
3/4	15,501–18,000
1/2	18,001–22,000
1/4	22,001–26,000
1/10	26,001–40,000
None	40,001 or more

Penalties etc: standard scale

(*Criminal Justice Act* 1982, s. 37)

Level on the scale	From 1 October 1992 £
1	200
2	500
3	1,000
4	2,500
5[1]	5,000

Note

[1]This is also the 'statutory maximum fine'.

Retail prices index

With effect from February 1987 the reference date to which the price level in each subsequent month is related was changed from 'January 1974 = 100' to 'January 1987 = 100' (with a base of January 1974 = 100, January 1987's RPI was 394.5). Movements in the RPI in the months after January 1987 are calculated with reference to January 1987 = 100. A new formula has been provided by the Department of Employment for calculating movements in the index over periods which span January 1987:

> 'The index for the later month (January 1987 = 100) is multiplied by the index for January 1987 (January 1974 = 100) and divided by the index for the earlier month (January 1974 = 100). 100 is subtracted to give the percentage change between the two months.'

Croner.CCH has prepared the following table in accordance with this formula:

	1982	1983	1984	1985	1986	1987	1988	1989	1990	1991
January		82.61	86.84	91.20	96.25	100.0	103.3	111.0	119.5	130.2
February		82.97	87.20	91.94	96.60	100.4	103.7	111.8	120.2	130.9
March	79.44	83.12	87.48	92.80	96.73	100.6	104.1	112.3	121.4	131.4
April	81.04	84.28	88.64	94.78	97.67	101.8	105.8	114.3	125.1	133.1
May	81.62	84.64	88.97	95.21	97.85	101.9	106.2	115.0	126.2	133.5
June	81.85	84.84	89.20	95.41	97.79	101.9	106.6	115.4	126.7	134.1
July	81.88	85.30	89.10	95.23	97.52	101.8	106.7	115.5	126.8	133.8
August	81.90	85.68	89.94	95.49	97.82	102.1	107.9	115.8	128.1	134.1
September	81.85	86.06	90.11	95.44	98.30	102.4	108.4	116.6	129.3	134.6
October	82.26	86.36	90.67	95.59	98.45	102.9	109.5	117.5	130.3	135.1
November	82.66	86.67	90.95	95.92	99.29	103.4	110.0	118.5	130.0	135.6
December	82.51	86.89	90.87	96.05	99.62	103.3	110.3	118.8	129.9	135.7

	1992	1993	1994	1995	1996	1997	1998	1999	2000
January	135.6	137.9	141.3	146.0	150.2	154.4	159.5	163.4	166.6
February	136.3	138.8	142.1	146.9	150.9	155.0	160.3	163.7	167.5
March	136.7	139.3	142.5	147.5	151.5	155.4	160.8	164.1	168.4
April	138.8	140.6	144.2	149.0	152.6	156.3	162.6	165.2	
May	139.3	141.1	144.7	149.6	152.9	156.9	163.5	165.6	
June	139.3	141.0	144.7	149.8	153.0	157.5	163.4	165.6	
July	138.8	140.7	144.0	149.1	152.4	157.5	163.0	165.1	
August	138.9	141.3	144.7	149.9	153.1	158.5	163.7	165.5	
September	139.4	141.9	145.0	150.6	153.8	159.3	164.4	166.2	
October	139.9	141.8	145.2	149.8	153.8	159.5	164.5	166.5	
November	139.7	141.6	145.3	149.8	153.9	159.6	164.4	166.7	
December	139.2	141.9	146.0	150.7	154.4	160.0	164.4	167.3	

The indexation factors are on p. 82.

Foreign exchange rates

Country	Unit of currency	*Average* for year to — 31 December 1998		31 March 1999	
		Currency units per £1	Sterling value of currency unit (£)	Currency units per £1	Sterling value of currency unit (£)
Algeria	Algerian Dinar	D.A. 97.8645	0.010218	D.A. 99.2018	0.01008
Argentina	Peso	$ 1.658	0.60314	$ 1.6539	0.60463
Australia	Australian Dollar	$A. 2.638	0.37908	$A. 2.6643	0.37533
Austria	Austrian Schilling	S. 20.5069	0.0487641	S. 20.2487	0.049386
Bahrain	Bahrain Dinar	B.D. 0.6254	1.59898	B.D. 0.6239	1.60282
Bangladesh	Taka	Tk. 77.9876	0.012823	Tk. 78.6191	0.012719
Barbados	Barbados Dollar	B.D.$ 3.3458	0.29888	B.D.$ 3.334	0.29994
Belgium	Belgian Franc	B.F. 60.1307	0.016630	B.F. 59.3682	0.016844
Bolivia	Boliviano	$.B. 9.1699	0.10905	$.B. 9.2559	0.10804
Botswana	Pula	P. 7.0147	0.14256	P. 7.2987	0.13701
Brazil	Real	R$ 1.9252	0.51943	R$ 2.1975	0.45506
Brunei	Brunei Dollar	$ 2.7657	0.36157	$ 2.7821	0.35944
Burma	Burmese Kyat	K. 10.3702	0.096430	K. 10.3445	0.096669
Burundi	Burundi Franc	Fbu 733.8387	0.0013627	Fbu 775.3835	0.0012897
Canada	Canadian Dollar	Can. $ 2.4588	0.40670	Can. $ 2.4873	0.40204
Cayman Islands	C.I. Dollar	CI $ 1.3762	0.72664	CI $ 1.3714	0.72918
Chile	Chilean Peso	Ch. $ 764.0855	0.0013088	Ch. $ 777.2736	0.0012865
China	Yuan	RMBY 13.7424	0.0727675	RMBY 13.6737	0.073133
Colombia	Colombian Peso	Col. $ 2367.175	0.00042244	Col. $ 2451.284	0.00040795
Congo Dem. Rep (Zaire)	Congolese Franc	224147.7	0.0000044613	223581.9	0.0000044726
Costa Rica	Colon	C 427.8467	0.0023373	C 436.6955	0.0022899
Cuba	Cuban Peso	Po 38.1782	0.026193	Po 37.9873	0.026325
Cyprus	Cyprus Pound	£C 0.8596	1.163332	£C 0.8521	1.17357
Czech Republic	Koruna	KC 53.3515	0.018744	KC 53.0363	0.018855
Denmark	Danish Kroner	D. Kr. 11.1015	0.090078	D. Kr. 10.9556	0.091278
Ecuador	Sucre	S/. 9258.9275	0.00010804	S/. 11008.15	0.000090842
Egypt	Egyptian Pound	LE 5.6636	0.17657	LE 5.6512	0.17695
El Salvador	Colon	C 14.5292	0.068827	C 14.4518	0.069196
Ethiopia	Ethiopian Birr	Br. 11.472	0.087169	Br. 11.5096	0.086884
European Union	Euro	1.4783 (ECU)	0.67645 (ECU)	1.4647	0.68273
Fiji Islands'	Fiji Dollar	F$ 3.3017	0.30287	F$ 3.3113	0.30199
Finland	Finnish Markka	Fmk. 8.8624	0.11284	Fmk. 8.7562	0.1142
France	French Franc	F 9.7681	0.10237	F 9.6473	0.10366
French Cty/Africa	CFA Franc	CFAF 979.1458	0.0010213	CFAF 967.5958	0.0010335
French Pacific Is.	CFP Franc	CFPF 177.7411	0.0056262	CFPF 175.5382	0.0056968
Gambia	Dalasi	D 17.0422	0.058678	D 17.3619	0.057597
Germany	Deutschmark	DM 2.9147	0.34309	DM 2.878	0.34746
Ghana	Ghanaian Cedi	C. 3846.755	0.00025996	C. 3869.185	0.00025845
Greece	Greek Drachma	Dr. 489.8869	0.0020413	Dr. 486.6462	0.0020549
Grenada & Windward Isles	East Caribbean Dollar	EC$. 4.4788	0.2232741	EC$. 4.4677	0.22383
Guyana	Guyanese Dollar	G$ 244.0337	0.0040978	G$ 249.2911	0.0040114
Honduras	Lempira	L 22.3154	0.0448121	L 22.518	0.044409
Hong Kong	H. K. Dollar	H.K.$ 12.8378	0.0778995	H.K.$ 12.8158	0.078029
Hungary	Forint	Ft 357.4845	0.0027973	Ft 363.4616	0.0027513
Iceland	Icelandic Krona	ISK 117.9762	0.0084763	ISK 117.0532	0.0085431
India	Indian Rupee	Re. 68.432	0.014613	Re. 69.5958	0.014369
Indonesia	Indonesian Rupiah	Rp. 16894	0.000059193	Rp. 16511.01	0.000060566
Iran	Iranian Rial	RLS 4976.34	0.000200951	RLS 4964	0.00020145
Iraq	Iraqi Dinar	ID 0.5157	1.93911	ID 0.5144	1.944012
Irish Republic	Irish Punt	Ir.£ 1.1635	0.85948	Ir.£ 1.1529	0.86738

Country	Unit of currency	*Average* for year to —			
		31 December 1998		31 March 1999	
		Currency units per £1	Sterling value of currency unit (£)	Currency units per £1	Sterling value of currency unit (£)
Israel	Shekel	NIS 6.3147	0.15836	NIS 6.4948	0.15397
Italy	Italian Lira	Lit. 2876.52	0.00034764	Lit. 2843.76	0.00035165
Jamaica	Jamaican Dollar	J$ 59.378	0.016841	J$ 60.0323	0.016658
Japan	Japanese Yen	Y 216.6834	0.00461503	Y 211.499	0.0047282
Jordan	Jordanian Dinar	JD 1.1796	0.847745	JD 1.1771	0.84955
Kenya	Kenyan Shilling	K Sh. 100.1734	0.0099827	K Sh. 100.8518	0.0099155
Korea (South)	Won	W 2269.7583	0.00044058	W 2133.946	0.000468862
Kuwait	Kuwaiti Dinar	KD 0.5057	1.97746	KD 0.5036	1.9857
Laos	New Kip	KN 4477.095	0.00022336	KN 5453.88	0.00018336
Lebanon	Lebanese Pound	LL 2515.233	0.00039758	LL 2501.539	0.00039975
Libya	Libyan Dinar	LD 0.6447	1.55111	LD 0.6703	1.49187
Luxembourg	Luxembourg Franc	Lf. 60.1307	0.016630	Lf. 59.3713	0.016843
Malawi	Malawi Kwacha	NK 52.1602	0.019172	NK 60.5949	0.016503
Malaysia	Ringgit	M$ 6.477	0.15439	M$ 6.4056	0.156113
Malta	Maltese Pound	Lm. 0.6449	1.55063	Lm. 0.6400	1.5625
Mauritius	Mauritian Rupee	Mau. Re. 39.7329	0.025168	Mau. Re. 40.4902	0.024697
Mexico	Mexican Peso	N$ 15.2139	0.065729	N$ 15.8026	0.063281
Morocco	Dirham	DH 15.9401	0.062735	DH 15.7773	0.063382
Nepal	Nepalese Rupee	N.Re. 99.6421	0.010036	N.Re. 101,4974	0.0098525
Netherlands	Neth. Guilder	f. 3.2854	0.30438	f. 3.2438	0.30828
N'nd Antilles	Antilles Guilder	Naf. 2.9713	0.33655	Na.f. 2.9546	0.33846
New Zealand	N.Z. Dollar	$NZ 3.0946	0.32314	$NZ 3.1402	0.31845
Nicaragua	Gold Cordoba	GC$ 17.05	0.058651	GC$ 17.4486	0.057311
Nigeria	Nigerian Naira	N. 36.3062	0.027544	N. 40.8369	0.024488
Norway	Norwegian Krone	N. Kr. 12.5117	0.079925	N. Kr. 12.5348	0.079778
Oman, Sultanate of	Rial Omani	RO 0.6387	1.56568	RO 0.6371	1.56961
Pakistan	Pakistani Rupee	P.Re. 77.9532	0.012828	P.Re. 80.1179	0.012482
Papua New Guinea	Kina	K 3.4923	0.28634	K 3.6339	0.27519
Paraguay	Guarani	G 4488.0871	0.00022281	G 4650.0563	0.00021505
Peru	New Sol	S 4.8575	0.20587	S 5.0689	0.19728
Philippines	Philippine Peso	P 67.8068	0.014748	P 65.6731	0.015227
Poland	Zloty	Zl 5.8184	0.17187	Zl 5.9455	0.16819
Portugal	Portuguese Escudo	Esc. 298.5344	0.0033497	Esc. 294.9011	0.003391
Qatar	Qatar Riyal	QR 6.0411	0.16553	QR 6.0242	0.165997
Romania	Leu	L 14935.4667	0.000066955	L 16801.7	0.000059518
Russia	Rouble (Market Rate)	17.6101	0.056786	24.9644	0.040057
Rwanda	Rwanda Franc	RF 538.8919	0.0018557	RF 525.5502	0.0019028
Saudi Arabia	Saudi Riyal	S.Rls 6.2222	0.16071	S.Rls 6.2069	0.161111
Seychelles	Seychelles Rupee	SR 8.7357	0.11447	SR 8.7682	0.11405
Sierra Leone	Leone	Le. 2083.987	0.00047985	Le. 2358.464	0.000424005
Singapore	Singapore Dollar	S$ 2.7692	0.36112	S$ 2.7791	0.35983
Solomon Islands	Sol. Islands Dollar	SI$ 7.9247	0.126188	SI$ 7.9434	0.12589
Somali Republic	Somali Schilling	SO. SH 4348.9917	0.00022994	SO. SH 4327.245	0.000231094
South Africa	Rand	R 9.1681	0.109074	R 9.6233	0.10391
Spain and Balearic Isles	Spanish Peseta	Ptas. 247.4537	0.00404412	Ptas. 244.5556	0.00408905
Sri Lanka	Sri Lanka Rupee	SLRe. 107.5062	0.0093018	SLRe. 110.1795	0.0090761
Sudan	Sudanese Dinar	LSd. 289.0171	0.0034600	LSd. 301.7498	0.003314
Surinam	Surinam Guilder	Sf. 665.6281	0.0015023	Sf. 662.2998	0.00150989
Swaziland	Lilangeli	L 9.2103	0.10857	L 9.6606	0.103513
Sweden	Swedish Krona	S.Kr. 13.1769	0.07589	S.Kr. 13.1419	0.076092
Switzerland	Swiss Franc	SwF 2.4011	0.41648	SwF 2.376	0.42088
Syria	Syrian Pound	LS 68.6522	0.014566	LS 70.0802	0.014269
Taiwan	New Taiwan Dollar	NT$ 55.4635	0.01803	NT$ 55.1962	0.018117
Tanzania	Tanzanian Schilling	T.Sh. 1081.67	0.00092449	T.Sh. 1099.416	0.000909574

Country	Unit of currency	Average for year to — 31 December 1998 Currency units per £1	31 December 1998 Sterling value of currency unit (£)	31 March 1999 Currency units per £1	31 March 1999 Sterling value of currency unit (£)
Thailand	Thai Baht	B. 68.2186	0.014659	B. 64.3246	0.015546
Tonga Islands	Pa Anga	T$ 2.6455	0.37800038	T$ 2.6829	0.3273
Trinidad & Tobago	Trinidad & Tobago Dollar	TT$ 10.3313	0.096793	TT$ 10.322	0.09688
Tunisia	Tunisian Dollar	D. 1.8879	0.52969	D. 1.8719	0.53422
Turkey	Turkish Lire	LT 436113.253	0.0000022930	LT 483958.502	0.0000020663
Uganda	Ugandan Schilling	U.Sh. 2041.597	0.00048981	U.Sh. 2131	0.00046926
United Arab Emirates	U.A.E. Dirham	Dh. 6.0927	0.16413	Dh. 6.0776	0.16454
Uruguay	Uruguayan Peso/	$17.3546	0.057622	$17.6704	0.056592
USA	US Dollar	US$ 1.6573	0.60339	US$ 1.6542	0.604522
Venezuela	Ven. Bolivar	Bs. 908.8414	0.0011	Bs. 931.5492	0.0010735
Vietnam	Dong	VND 22094.9167	0.000045259	VND 22451.46	0.0000445405
Yemen	Yemen Rial	YRL 218.2828	0.0045812	YRL 222.6623	0.00449111
Zambia	Zambian Kwacha	K 3177.2307	0.00031474	K 3508.3228	0.00028504
Zimbabwe	Zimbabwe Dollar	Z$ 39.4382	0.025356	Z$ 48.2683	0.020718

Table of spot rates on 31 December 1998 and 31 March 1999

Country	Unit of currency	31 December 1998 Currency units per £1	31 December 1998 Sterling value of currency unit (£)	31 March 1999 Currency units per £1	31 March 1999 Sterling value of currency unit (£)
Australia	Australian Dollar	$A. 2.7126	0.36865	$A. 2.5563	0.39119
Austria	Austrian Schilling	S. 19.4965	0.051291	S. 20.5755	0.0486014
Belgium	Belgian Franc	B.F. 57.1561	0.017496	B.F. 60.3193	0.0165784
Canada	Canadian Dollar	Can.$ 2.5555	0.391313	Can.$ 2.4421	0.409483
Denmark	Danish Kroner	D. Kr. 10.589	0.094438	D. Kr. 11.1137	0.089979
European Union	Euro	ECU 1.4169	ECU 0.70577	ECU 1.4953	ECU 0.66876
France	French Franc	F 9.294	0.107596	F 9.8084	F 0.1019534
Germany	Deutschmark	DM 2.7711	0.360868	DM 2.9245	0.3419388
Hong Kong	H.K. Dollar	H.K.$ 12.8895	0.077583	H.K.$ 12.5101	0.0799354
Irish Repubiic	Irish Punt	Ir.£ 1.1159	0.896134	Ir.£ 1.776	0.8491848
Italy	Italian Lira	Lit. 2743.43	0.000364507	Lit. 2895.26	0.000345392
Japan	Japanese Yen	Y 187.671	0.0053285	Y 191.182	0.0052306
Luxembourg	Luxembourg Franc	Lf. 57.1561	0.017496	Lf. 60.3193	0.0165784
Netherlands	Neth. Guilder	f. 3.1224	0.3202665	f. 3.2952	0.3034717
Norway	Norwegian Krone	N. Kr. 12.6761	0.078889	N. Kr. 12.4765	0.0801507
Portugal	Portuguese Escudo	Esc. 284.055	0.00352045	Esc. 299.776	0.0033358
South Africa	Rand	R 9.7875	0.1021711	R 9.9845	0.1001552
Spain and Balearic Isles	Spanish Peseta	Ptas. 235.746	0.0042419	Ptas. 248.793	0.0040194
Sweden	Swedish Krone	Skr. 13.486	0.07415097	S.Kr. 13.2744	0.07533298
Switzerland	Swiss Franc	SwF 2.2852	0.437598	Sw.F. 2.3894	0.4185151
USA	US Dollar	US$ 1.6638	0.60103378	US$ 1.6143	0.6194635

Double tax treaties

The UK has concluded a large number of tax treaties with other countries to avoid international double taxation and to prevent fiscal evasion. Tax treaties covering all usual areas of possible double taxation (comprehensive agreements) have been made, and those currently in force are indicated below by the letter 'C' in brackets. The table also notes agreements relating to shipping and air transport profits (S/A); air transport profits only (A); estates, inheritance and gifts (E/I/G); and social security contributions (SS).

Algeria (A)
Antigua and Barbuda (C)
Argentina (C)
Armenia (C)[1]
Australia (C/SS)
Austria (C/SS)
Azerbaijan (C)
Bangladesh (C)
Barbados (C/SS)
Belarus (C/A)[1]
Belgium (C/SS)
Belize (C)
Bolivia (C)
Botswana (C)
Brazil (S/A)
Brunei (C)
Bulgaria (C)
Burma (Myanmar) (C)
Cameroon (A)
Canada (C)
China (C/A)
Croatia (C)[2]
Cyprus (C/SS)
Czech Republic (C)
Denmark (C/SS)
Egypt (C)
Estonia (C)
Ethiopia (A)
Falkland Islands (C)
Fiji (C)
Finland (C/SS)
France (includes Guadeloupe, Guyane, Martinique and Réunion) (C/E/SS)
Gambia (C)
Georgia (C)[1]
Germany (C/SS)
Ghana (C)
Greece (C)
Grenada (C)
Guernsey (includes Alderney, Herm and Lithou) (C/SS)
Guyana (C)
Hong Kong SAR(A)
Hungary (C)
Iceland (C/SS)
India (C/E)
Indonesia (C)
Iran (A)
Irish Republic (C/E/I/G/SS)
Isle of Man (C/SS)
Israel (C/SS)
Italy (C/E/SS)
Ivory Coast (C)
Jamaica (C/SS)
Japan (C)
Jersey (C/SS)
Jordan (S/A)
Kazakstan (C)
Kenya (C)
Kiribati & Tuvalu (C)
Korean Republic (C)
Kuwait (C)
Kyrgystan (C)[1]
Latvia (C)
Lebanon (S/A)
Lesotho (C)
Luxembourg (C/SS)
Macedonia (C)[2]
Malawi (C)
Malaysia (C)
Malta (C/SS)
Mauritius (C/SS)
Mexico (C)
Moldova (C)[1]
Mongolia (C)
Montserrat (C)
Morocco (C)
Namibia (C)
Netherlands (C/E/I/G/SS)
New Zealand (C)
Nigeria (C)
Norway (C/SS)
Oman (C)
Pakistan (C/E)
Papua New Guinea (C)
Philippines (C/SS)
Poland (C)
Portugal (C/SS)
Romania (C)
Russian Federation (C)
St. Christopher (St. Kitts) & Nevis (C)
Saudi Arabia (A)
Sierra Leone (C)
Singapore (C)
Slovak Republic (C)
Slovenia (C)[2]
Solomon Islands (C)
South Africa (C/E/I/G)
Spain (C/SS)
Sri Lanka (C)
Sudan (C)
Swaziland (C)
Sweden (C/E/I/G/SS)
Switzerland (C/E/SS)
Tajikistan (C)[1]
Thailand (C)
Trinidad and Tobago (C)
Tunisia (C)
Turkey (C/SS)
Tuvaln (C)
Turkmenistan (C)[1]
Uganda (C)
Ukraine (C)
USA (C/E/I/G/SS)
Uzbekistan (C/A)
Venezuela (C)
Vietnam (C)
Yugoslavia (C/SS)[2]
Zaire (S/A)
Zambia (C)
Zimbabwe (C)

Notes

(1) See SP 3/92 for the status of the Convention of 31 July 1985 with the former USSR.
(2) See SP 6/93 for the status of the Convention of 5 November 1981 with the former Yugoslavia.

The reciprocal social security arrangements made with EU member states have all, with the exception of parts of the Orders relating to Germany, been superseded by EC Regulation 1408/71 (as codified and amended). See Leaflet SA 29 for social security rights in the EU.

Clearance procedures

Subject	Statutory reference etc.	Application submitted to:
Maintenance funds for historic buildings	IHTA 1984, Sch. 4, para. 1	Inland Revenue Capital Taxes Office Ferrers House PO Box 38 Castle Meadow Road Nottingham NG2 1BB
Demergers	ICTA 1988, s. 215	Inland Revenue Central Registry Room 28, New Wing Somerset House London WC2R 1LB
Purchase by company of own shares	ICTA 1988, s. 225	Inland Revenue Central Registry Room 28, New Wing Somerset House London WC2R 1LB
Transactions in securities	ICTA 1988, s. 707	Inland Revenue Section 703 Group Special Investigations Section 2 Third Floor South West Wing Bush House, Strand London WC2B 4QN
Offshore funds: certification as distributing fund	ICTA 1988, s. 760	Inland Revenue Technical Division (Offshore Funds) Room 208 St. John's House Merton Road Bootle Merseyside L69 9BB
Certain issues of shares/ debentures by, or transfers of shares/debentures of, a non-resident company	ICTA 1988, s. 765	The Secretary HM Treasury (AP) Parliament Street London SW1P 3AG
Artificial transactions in land	ICTA 1988, s. 776	Inspector of Taxes
Profit sharing schemes Savings-related share option schemes Employee share option schemes	ICTA 1988, Sch. 9, para. 1	Employee Share Schemes Unit Inland Revenue Savings and Investment Division (Employee Share Schemes) First Floor South West Wing Bush House, Strand London WC2B 4RD

Subject	Statutory reference etc.	Application submitted to:
Company reconstructions and amalgamations: capital gains tax	TCGA 1992, s. 138	Inland Revenue Capital Gains Clearance Section Sapphire House 550 Streetsbrook Road Solihull West Midlands B91 1QU
Company reconstructions and amalgamations: transfer of assets	TCGA 1992, s. 139	Inland Revenue Capital Gains Clearance Section Sapphire House 550 Streetsbrook Road Solihull West Midlands B91 1QU
Transfer of trades between member states	TCGA 1992, s. 140B(2), 140D(2)	Inland Revenue Capital Gains Clearance Section Sapphire House 550 Streetsbrook Road Solihull West Midlands B91 1QU
Withholding tax on non-resident entertainers and sportsmen	SI 1987/530	Inland Revenue Foreign Entertainers Unit 2nd Floor Princes Gate Homer Road Solihull West Midlands B91 3SA
Employee share ownership trusts	Inland Revenue press releases, 9 May 1990 and 14 December 1990	Inland Revenue Business Profits Division (Employee Share Schemes) Room IIIA New Wing Somerset House London WC2R 1LB

Recognised stock exchanges

'The Stock Exchange' (strictly known as 'The International Stock Exchange of the United Kingdom and the Republic of Ireland Ltd') is a 'recognised stock exchange'; the stock exchanges of the following countries have also been designated by the Board of Inland Revenue as 'recognised stock exchanges'. Where there is no specific or unified exchange shown there is included any exchange recognised by the laws of that country (ICTA 1988, s. 841; TCGA 1992, s. 288(1)):

Australia (unified) Austria Belgium Brazil (Rio de Janeiro, São Paulo) Canada Denmark (Copenhagen) Finland (Helsinki) France Germany Greece (Athens)	Hong Kong Ireland[(1)] Italy Japan Korea Luxembourg Malaysia (Kuala Lumpur) Mexico Netherlands New Zealand (unified) Norway	Portugal Singapore (unified) South Africa (Johannesburg) Spain Sri Lanka (Colombo) Sweden (Stockholm) Switzerland (Zurich, Basle, Geneva) Thailand United States

Note

(1) Since 25 March 1973 the stock exchange in Ireland has been included within 'The Stock Exchange'.

Recognised futures exchanges

The following futures exchanges have been designated by the Board of Inland Revenue as 'recognised futures exchanges' (TCGA 1992, s. 288(6))[(1)]:

Date	Exchange
From 22 March 1992	London International Financial Futures and Options Exchange (LIFFE)[(2)]
From 6 August 1985	International Petroleum Exchange of London London Metal Exchange London Wool Terminal Market
From 12 December 1985	London Gold Market London Silver Market
From 19 December 1986	Chicago Mercantile Exchange Philadelphia Board of Trade New York Mercantile Exchange
From 24 April 1987	Chicago Board of Trade
From 29 July 1987	Montreal Exchange Mid-America Commodity Exchange
From 15 December 1987	Hong Kong Futures Exchange New York Coffee Sugar and Cocoa Exchange
From 25 August 1988	Commodity Exchange, Inc (COMEX) Citrus Associates of the New York Cotton Exchange Inc New York Cotton Exchange
From 31 October 1988	Sydney Futures Exchange Ltd
From 18 March 1992	OM Stockholm London Commodity Exchange[(3)] OMLX (formerly OM London)

Note

(1) When the Board recognises a futures exchange this is announced in the *London Gazette*.

(2) The London International Financial Futures Exchange and the London Traded Options Market merged on 22 March 1992, forming the London International Financial Futures and Options Exchange (LIFFE).

(3) The following futures exchanges, which are recognised from 6 August 1985, are now part of the London Commodity Exchange: Baltic International Freight Futures Exchange; London Cocoa Terminal Market; London Coffee Terminal Market; London Futures and Options Exchange; London Grain Futures Market; London Meat Futures Market; London Potato Futures Market; London Rubber Market; London Soya Bean Meal Futures Market; London Sugar Terminal Market. The name of the London International Financial Futures Exchange changed to London Commodity Exchange from 1 July 1993.

Recognised clearing systems

The following clearing systems have been designated by the Board of Inland Revenue as 'recognised clearing systems' (ICTA 1988, s. 841A, for the purposes of s. 124(2)):

Country	Clearing system	Effective date
Belgium	Euroclear	26 July 1984
Luxembourg	Cedel	26 July 1984
United Kingdom	Bank of England European Settlements Office	16 August 1993
	First Chicago Clearing Centre	14 October 1988
United States	The Depository Trust Co	18 July 1995

Recognised investment exchanges

Regulations may designate 'recognised investment exchanges' within the meaning of the *Financial Services Act* 1986, s. 37(3) so that securities traded on such exchanges are treated in the same way for tax purposes as those traded on 'The Stock Exchange' (strictly known as 'The International Stock Exchange of the United Kingdom and the Republic of Ireland Ltd') (FA 1986, Sch. 18, para. 8; F(No. 2)A 1987, s. 73; ICTA 1988, s. 841(3)).

From 22 March 1992: London International Financial Futures Exchange (Administration and Management) (LIFFE (A & M)).

CAPITAL GAINS TAX

Reliefs etc., rates and thresholds

Tax year	Annual exempt amount		Chattel exemption (max sale proceeds)[1]	Rate	
	Individuals, PRs[2], trusts for mentally disabled[3] £	Other trusts[3] £	£	Individuals %	Trustees and PRs %
2000–2001	7,200	3,600	6,000	10/20/40[4]	34
1999–2000	7,100	3,550	6,000	20/40[4]	34
1998–99	6,800	3,400	6,000	20/23/40[4]	34[6]
1997–98	6,500	3,250	6,000	20/23/40[4]	23[5]
1996–97	6,300	3,150	6,000	20/24/40[4]	24[5]
1995–96	6,000	3,000	6,000	20/25/40[4]	25[5]
1994–95	5,800	2,900	6,000	20/25/40[4]	25[5]

Notes

[1] Where disposal proceeds exceed the exemption limit, marginal relief restricts any chargeable gain to $^{5}/_{3}$ of the excess. Where there is a loss and the proceeds are less than £6,000 the proceeds are deemed to be £6,000.

[2] For year of death and next two years.

[3] Multiple trusts created by the same settlor: each attracts relief equal to the annual amount divided by the number of such trusts (subject to a minimum of 10% of the full annual amount).

[4] From 2000–2001, capital gains are taxed at the individual's marginal income tax rate. For 1999–2000, capital gains are taxed at 20% where the gains when added to total income are below the basic rate limit and 40% where they exceed that limit. Before 1999–2000, capital gains were taxed at the individual's marginal income tax rate.

[5] The rate of tax applicable to trustees of discretionary trusts is a flat rate of 34% for 1996–97 onwards (35% for 1993–94 to 1995–96).

[6] For 1998–99 onwards, the flat rate of 34% applicable to trusts also applies to all gains realised by trustees and personal representatives of deceased persons.

Due date for payment

(TCGA 1992, s. 7)

1997–98 onwards

See p. 10.

1995–96 and previous years

1 December following tax year in which gains accrued; or 30 days after issue of assessment (or determination/agreement of tax postponed) if later.

Reckonable date where tax postponed following appeal (TMA 1970, s. 86)
Later of:

- actual due and payable date if there had been no appeal against the assessment, and
- 1 June following 1 December after end of tax year in which gains accrued.

trt trt97b Mp 80—trt 120

Leases which are wasting assets

Restriction of allowable expenditure (TCGA 1992, s. 240 and Sch. 8, para. 1)

Fraction equal to $\frac{P(1) - P(3)}{P(1)}$ excluded from base cost,

and fraction equal to $\frac{P(2) - P(3)}{P(2)}$ excluded from other expenditure where:

P(1) = table percentage for duration of lease at time of acquisition (or 31 March 1982 where applicable);
P(2) = table percentage for duration of lease at time expenditure incurred; and
P(3) = table percentage for duration of lease at time of disposal.

Years	%	Monthly[1] increment	Years	%	Monthly[1] increment	Years	%	Monthly[1] increment
50 or more	100	—	33	90.280	.073	16	64.116	.196
49	99.657	.029	32	89.354	.077	15	61.617	.208
48	99.289	.031	31	88.371	.082	14	58.971	.221
47	98.902	.032	30	87.330	.087	13	56.167	.234
46	98.490	.034	29	86.226	.092	12	53.191	.247
45	98.059	.036	28	85.053	.098	11	50.038	.263
44	97.595	.039	27	83.816	.103	10	46.695	.279
43	97.107	.041	26	82.496	.110	9	43.154	.295
42	96.593	.043	25	81.100	.116	8	39.399	.313
41	96.041	.046	24	79.622	.123	7	35.414	.332
40	95.457	.049	23	78.055	.131	6	31.195	.352
39	94.842	.051	22	76.399	.138	5	26.722	.373
38	94.189	.054	21	74.635	.147	4	21.983	.395
37	93.497	.058	20	72.770	.155	3	16.959	.419
36	92.761	.061	19	70.791	.165	2	11.629	.444
35	91.981	.065	18	68.697	.175	1	5.983	.470
34	91.156	.069	17	66.470	.186	0	0	.499

Note

[1] Where duration is *not* an *exact* number of years, the table percentage for the whole number of years is increased by $^1/_{12}$ of the difference between that and the next highest percentage for each odd month. Fourteen odd days or more are rounded up and treated as a month; less than 14 odd days are ignored.

Indexation allowance

The retail prices index figures are on p. 71.
For a table showing the indexed rise concerning recent disposals, see below.

Capital gains tax: disposals after 5 April 1985 (31 March 1985 in the case of companies)

Allowance = Acquisition cost/31 March 1982 market value × $\frac{RD - RI}{RI}$

Where: RD = retail prices index for month in which disposal occurred; and
RI = retail prices index for either March 1982 or month in which acquisition occurred, whichever is the later.

Capital gains tax: disposals before 6 April 1985 (1 April 1985 in the case of companies)

Allowance = Acquisition cost × $\frac{RD - RI}{RI}$

Where: RD = retail prices index for month in which disposal occurred;
RI = retail prices index for either March 1982 or twelfth month after acquisition, whichever is the later.

Note

[1] Indexation allowance is restricted for disposals on or after 30 November 1993. The maximum allowance is limited to an amount equal to the unindexed gain and no allowance is available if there is an unindexed loss.

[2] Individuals within the charge to capital gains tax are not entitled to indexation allowance for any period after 1 April 1998.

RD Month (April 1999–March 2000) January 1987 = 100

RI Month	1999 April	May	June	July	Aug.	Sept.	Oct.	Nov.	Dec.	2000 Jan.	Feb.	Mar.
1982 *March*	1.079	1.085	1.085	1.078	1.083	1.092	1.096	1.098	1.106	1.097	1.108	1.120
April	1.039	1.043	1.043	1.037	1.042	1.051	1.055	1.057	1.064	1.056	1.067	1.078
May	1.024	1.029	1.029	1.023	1.028	1.036	1.040	1.042	1.050	1.041	1.052	1.063
June	1.018	1.023	1.023	1.017	1.022	1.031	1.034	1.037	1.044	1.035	1.046	1.057
July	1.018	1.023	1.023	1.016	1.021	1.030	1.034	1.036	1.043	1.035	1.046	1.057
Aug.	1.017	1.022	1.022	1.016	1.021	1.029	1.033	1.035	1.043	1.034	1.045	1.056
Sept.	1.018	1.023	1.023	1.017	1.022	1.031	1.034	1.037	1.044	1.035	1.046	1.057
Oct.	1.008	1.013	1.013	1.007	1.012	1.021	1.024	1.027	1.034	1.025	1.036	1.047
Nov.	0.999	1.003	1.003	0.997	1.002	1.011	1.014	1.017	1.024	1.015	1.026	1.037
Dec.	1.002	1.007	1.007	1.001	1.006	1.014	1.018	1.020	1.028	1.019	1.030	1.041
1983 *Jan.*	1.000	1.005	1.005	0.999	1.003	1.012	1.015	1.018	1.025	1.017	1.028	1.038
Feb.	0.991	0.996	0.996	0.990	0.995	1.003	1.007	1.009	1.016	1.008	1.019	1.030
March	0.988	0.992	0.992	0.986	0.991	1.000	1.003	1.006	1.013	1.004	1.015	1.026
April	0.960	0.965	0.965	0.959	0.964	0.972	0.975	0.978	0.985	0.977	0.987	0.998
May	0.952	0.957	0.957	0.951	0.955	0.964	0.967	0.970	0.977	0.968	0.979	0.990
June	0.947	0.952	0.952	0.946	0.951	0.959	0.962	0.965	0.972	0.964	0.974	0.985
July	0.937	0.941	0.941	0.936	0.940	0.948	0.952	0.954	0.961	0.953	0.964	0.974
Aug.	0.928	0.933	0.933	0.927	0.932	0.940	0.943	0.946	0.953	0.944	0.955	0.965
Sept.	0.920	0.924	0.924	0.918	0.923	0.931	0.935	0.937	0.944	0.936	0.946	0.957
Oct.	0.913	0.917	0.917	0.912	0.916	0.924	0.928	0.930	0.937	0.929	0.939	0.950
Nov.	0.906	0.911	0.911	0.905	0.910	0.918	0.921	0.923	0.930	0.922	0.933	0.943
Dec.	0.901	0.906	0.906	0.900	0.905	0.913	0.916	0.918	0.925	0.917	0.928	0.938
1984 *Jan.*	0.902	0.907	0.907	0.901	0.906	0.914	0.917	0.920	0.926	0.918	0.929	0.939
Feb.	0.895	0.899	0.899	0.893	0.898	0.906	0.909	0.912	0.919	0.911	0.921	0.931
March	0.888	0.893	0.893	0.887	0.892	0.900	0.903	0.906	0.912	0.904	0.915	0.925
April	0.864	0.868	0.868	0.863	0.867	0.875	0.878	0.881	0.887	0.879	0.890	0.900
May	0.857	0.861	0.861	0.856	0.860	0.868	0.871	0.874	0.880	0.872	0.883	0.893
June	0.852	0.856	0.856	0.851	0.855	0.863	0.867	0.869	0.876	0.868	0.878	0.888
July	0.854	0.859	0.859	0.853	0.857	0.865	0.869	0.871	0.878	0.870	0.880	0.890
Aug.	0.837	0.841	0.841	0.836	0.840	0.848	0.851	0.854	0.860	0.852	0.862	0.872
Sept.	0.833	0.838	0.838	0.832	0.837	0.844	0.848	0.850	0.857	0.849	0.859	0.869
Oct.	0.822	0.826	0.826	0.821	0.825	0.833	0.836	0.839	0.845	0.837	0.847	0.857
Nov.	0.816	0.821	0.821	0.815	0.820	0.827	0.831	0.833	0.839	0.832	0.842	0.852
Dec.	0.818	0.822	0.822	0.817	0.821	0.829	0.832	0.834	0.841	0.833	0.843	0.853
1985 *Jan.*	0.811	0.816	0.816	0.810	0.815	0.822	0.826	0.828	0.834	0.827	0.837	0.846
Feb.	0.797	0.801	0.801	0.796	0.800	0.808	0.811	0.813	0.820	0.812	0.822	0.832

RD Month (April 1999–March 2000) January 1987 = 100

RI Month	1999 April	May	June	July	Aug.	Sept.	Oct.	Nov.	Dec.	2000 Jan.	Feb.	Mar.
1985 March	0.780	0.784	0.784	0.779	0.783	0.791	0.794	0.796	0.803	0.795	0.805	0.815
April	0.743	0.747	0.747	0.742	0.746	0.754	0.757	0.759	0.765	0.758	0.767	0.777
May	0.735	0.739	0.739	0.734	0.738	0.746	0.749	0.751	0.757	0.750	0.759	0.769
June	0.731	0.736	0.736	0.730	0.735	0.742	0.745	0.747	0.753	0.746	0.756	0.765
July	0.735	0.739	0.739	0.734	0.738	0.745	0.748	0.750	0.757	0.749	0.759	0.768
Aug.	0.730	0.734	0.734	0.729	0.733	0.741	0.744	0.746	0.752	0.745	0.754	0.764
Sept.	0.731	0.735	0.735	0.730	0.734	0.741	0.745	0.747	0.753	0.746	0.755	0.765
Oct.	0.728	0.732	0.732	0.727	0.731	0.739	0.742	0.744	0.750	0.743	0.752	0.762
Nov.	0.722	0.726	0.726	0.721	0.725	0.733	0.736	0.738	0.744	0.737	0.746	0.756
Dec.	0.720	0.724	0.724	0.719	0.723	0.730	0.734	0.736	0.742	0.735	0.744	0.753
1986 Jan.	0.716	0.721	0.721	0.715	0.720	0.727	0.730	0.732	0.738	0.731	0.740	0.750
Feb.	0.710	0.714	0.714	0.709	0.713	0.720	0.724	0.726	0.732	0.725	0.734	0.743
March	0.708	0.712	0.712	0.707	0.711	0.718	0.721	0.723	0.730	0.722	0.732	0.741
April	0.691	0.696	0.696	0.690	0.695	0.702	0.705	0.707	0.713	0.706	0.715	0.724
May	0.688	0.692	0.692	0.687	0.691	0.699	0.702	0.704	0.710	0.703	0.712	0.721
June	0.689	0.693	0.693	0.688	0.692	0.699	0.703	0.705	0.711	0.704	0.713	0.722
July	0.694	0.698	0.698	0.693	0.697	0.704	0.707	0.709	0.716	0.708	0.718	0.727
Aug.	0.689	0.693	0.693	0.688	0.692	0.699	0.702	0.704	0.710	0.703	0.712	0.722
Sept.	0.681	0.685	0.685	0.680	0.684	0.691	0.694	0.696	0.702	0.695	0.704	0.713
Oct.	0.678	0.682	0.682	0.677	0.681	0.688	0.691	0.693	0.699	0.692	0.701	0.710
Nov.	0.664	0.668	0.668	0.663	0.667	0.674	0.677	0.679	0.685	0.678	0.687	0.696
Dec.	0.658	0.662	0.662	0.657	0.661	0.668	0.671	0.673	0.679	0.672	0.681	0.690
1987 Jan.	0.652	0.656	0.656	0.651	0.655	0.662	0.665	0.667	0.673	0.666	0.675	0.684
Feb.	0.645	0.649	0.649	0.644	0.648	0.655	0.658	0.660	0.666	0.659	0.668	0.677
March	0.642	0.646	0.646	0.641	0.645	0.652	0.655	0.657	0.663	0.656	0.665	0.674
April	0.623	0.627	0.627	0.622	0.626	0.633	0.636	0.638	0.643	0.637	0.645	0.654
May	0.621	0.625	0.625	0.620	0.624	0.631	0.634	0.636	0.642	0.635	0.644	0.653
June	0.621	0.625	0.625	0.620	0.624	0.631	0.634	0.636	0.642	0.635	0.644	0.653
July	0.623	0.627	0.627	0.622	0.626	0.633	0.636	0.638	0.643	0.637	0.645	0.654
Aug.	0.618	0.622	0.622	0.617	0.621	0.628	0.631	0.633	0.639	0.632	0.641	0.649
Sept.	0.613	0.617	0.617	0.612	0.616	0.623	0.626	0.628	0.634	0.627	0.636	0.645
Oct.	0.605	0.609	0.609	0.604	0.608	0.615	0.618	0.620	0.626	0.619	0.628	0.637
Nov.	0.598	0.602	0.602	0.597	0.601	0.607	0.610	0.612	0.618	0.611	0.620	0.629
Dec.	0.599	0.603	0.603	0.598	0.602	0.609	0.612	0.614	0.620	0.613	0.621	0.630
1988 Jan.	0.599	0.603	0.603	0.598	0.602	0.609	0.612	0.614	0.620	0.613	0.621	0.630
Feb.	0.593	0.597	0.597	0.592	0.596	0.603	0.606	0.608	0.613	0.607	0.615	0.624

RD Month (April 1999–March 2000) January 1987 = 100

RI Month	1999 *April*	*May*	*June*	*July*	*Aug.*	*Sept.*	*Oct.*	*Nov.*	*Dec.*	2000 *Jan.*	*Feb.*	*Mar.*
1988 *March*	0.587	0.591	0.591	0.586	0.590	0.597	0.599	0.601	0.607	0.600	0.609	0.618
April	0.561	0.565	0.565	0.560	0.564	0.571	0.574	0.576	0.581	0.575	0.583	0.592
May	0.556	0.559	0.559	0.555	0.558	0.565	0.568	0.570	0.575	0.569	0.577	0.586
June	0.550	0.553	0.553	0.549	0.553	0.559	0.562	0.564	0.569	0.563	0.571	0.580
July	0.548	0.552	0.552	0.547	0.551	0.558	0.560	0.562	0.568	0.561	0.570	0.578
Aug.	0.531	0.535	0.535	0.530	0.534	0.540	0.543	0.545	0.551	0.544	0.552	0.561
Sept.	0.524	0.528	0.528	0.523	0.527	0.533	0.536	0.538	0.543	0.537	0.545	0.554
Oct.	0.509	0.512	0.512	0.508	0.511	0.518	0.521	0.522	0.528	0.521	0.530	0.538
Nov.	0.502	0.505	0.505	0.501	0.505	0.511	0.514	0.515	0.521	0.515	0.523	0.531
Dec.	0.498	0.501	0.501	0.497	0.500	0.507	0.510	0.511	0.517	0.510	0.519	0.527
1989 *Jan.*	0.488	0.492	0.492	0.487	0.491	0.497	0.500	0.502	0.507	0.501	0.509	0.517
Feb.	0.478	0.481	0.481	0.477	0.480	0.487	0.489	0.491	0.496	0.490	0.498	0.506
March	0.471	0.475	0.475	0.470	0.474	0.480	0.483	0.484	0.490	0.484	0.492	0.500
April	0.445	0.449	0.449	0.444	0.448	0.454	0.457	0.458	0.464	0.458	0.465	0.473
May	0.437	0.440	0.440	0.436	0.439	0.445	0.448	0.450	0.455	0.449	0.457	0.464
June	0.432	0.435	0.435	0.431	0.434	0.440	0.443	0.445	0.450	0.444	0.451	0.459
July	0.430	0.434	0.434	0.429	0.433	0.439	0.442	0.443	0.448	0.442	0.450	0.458
Aug.	0.427	0.430	0.430	0.426	0.429	0.435	0.438	0.440	0.445	0.439	0.446	0.454
Sept.	0.417	0.420	0.420	0.416	0.419	0.425	0.428	0.430	0.435	0.429	0.437	0.444
Oct.	0.406	0.409	0.409	0.405	0.409	0.414	0.417	0.419	0.424	0.418	0.426	0.433
Nov.	0.394	0.397	0.397	0.393	0.397	0.403	0.405	0.407	0.412	0.406	0.414	0.421
Dec.	0.391	0.394	0.394	0.390	0.393	0.399	0.402	0.403	0.408	0.402	0.410	0.418
1990 *Jan.*	0.382	0.386	0.386	0.382	0.385	0.391	0.393	0.395	0.400	0.394	0.402	0.409
Feb.	0.374	0.378	0.378	0.374	0.377	0.383	0.385	0.387	0.392	0.386	0.394	0.401
March	0.361	0.364	0.364	0.360	0.363	0.369	0.371	0.373	0.378	0.372	0.380	0.387
April	0.321	0.324	0.324	0.320	0.323	0.329	0.331	0.333	0.337	0.332	0.339	0.346
May	0.309	0.312	0.312	0.308	0.311	0.317	0.319	0.321	0.326	0.320	0.327	0.334
June	0.304	0.307	0.307	0.303	0.306	0.312	0.314	0.316	0.320	0.315	0.322	0.329
July	0.303	0.306	0.306	0.302	0.305	0.311	0.313	0.315	0.319	0.314	0.321	0.328
Aug.	0.290	0.293	0.293	0.289	0.292	0.297	0.300	0.301	0.306	0.301	0.308	0.315
Sept.	0.278	0.281	0.281	0.277	0.280	0.285	0.288	0.289	0.294	0.288	0.295	0.302
Oct.	0.268	0.271	0.271	0.267	0.270	0.276	0.278	0.279	0.284	0.279	0.285	0.292
Nov.	0.271	0.274	0.274	0.270	0.273	0.278	0.281	0.282	0.287	0.282	0.288	0.295
Dec.	0.272	0.275	0.275	0.271	0.274	0.279	0.282	0.283	0.288	0.283	0.289	0.296
1991 *Jan.*	0.269	0.272	0.272	0.268	0.271	0.276	0.279	0.280	0.285	0.280	0.286	0.293
Feb.	0.262	0.265	0.265	0.261	0.264	0.270	0.272	0.273	0.278	0.273	0.280	0.286

RD Month (April 1999–March 2000) January 1987 = 100

	1999 *April*	*May*	*June*	*July*	*Aug.*	*Sept.*	*Oct.*	*Nov.*	*Dec.*	**2000** *Jan.*	*Feb.*	*Mar.*
RI Month												
1991 *March*	0.257	0.260	0.260	0.256	0.260	0.265	0.267	0.269	0.273	0.268	0.275	0.282
April	0.241	0.244	0.244	0.240	0.243	0.249	0.251	0.252	0.257	0.252	0.258	0.265
May	0.237	0.240	0.240	0.237	0.240	0.245	0.247	0.249	0.253	0.248	0.255	0.261
June	0.232	0.235	0.235	0.231	0.234	0.239	0.242	0.243	0.248	0.242	0.249	0.256
July	0.235	0.238	0.238	0.234	0.237	0.242	0.244	0.246	0.250	0.245	0.252	0.259
Aug.	0.232	0.235	0.235	0.231	0.234	0.239	0.242	0.243	0.248	0.242	0.249	0.256
Sept.	0.227	0.230	0.230	0.227	0.230	0.235	0.237	0.238	0.243	0.238	0.244	0.251
Oct.	0.223	0.226	0.226	0.222	0.225	0.230	0.232	0.234	0.238	0.233	0.240	0.246
Nov.	0.218	0.221	0.221	0.218	0.221	0.226	0.228	0.229	0.234	0.229	0.235	0.242
Dec.	0.217	0.220	0.220	0.217	0.220	0.225	0.227	0.228	0.233	0.228	0.234	0.241
1992 *Jan.*	0.218	0.221	0.221	0.218	0.221	0.226	0.228	0.229	0.234	0.229	0.235	0.242
Feb.	0.212	0.215	0.215	0.211	0.214	0.219	0.222	0.223	0.227	0.222	0.229	0.236
March	0.208	0.211	0.211	0.208	0.211	0.216	0.218	0.219	0.224	0.219	0.225	0.232
April	0.190	0.193	0.193	0.189	0.192	0.197	0.200	0.201	0.205	0.200	0.207	0.213
May	0.186	0.189	0.189	0.185	0.188	0.193	0.195	0.197	0.201	0.196	0.202	0.209
June	0.186	0.189	0.189	0.185	0.188	0.193	0.195	0.197	0.201	0.202	0.202	0.209
July	0.190	0.193	0.193	0.189	0.192	0.197	0.200	0.201	0.205	0.200	0.207	0.213
Aug.	0.189	0.192	0.192	0.189	0.192	0.197	0.199	0.200	0.204	0.199	0.206	0.212
Sept.	0.185	0.188	0.188	0.184	0.187	0.192	0.194	0.196	0.200	0.195	0.202	0.208
Oct.	0.181	0.184	0.184	0.180	0.183	0.188	0.190	0.192	0.196	0.191	0.197	0.204
Nov.	0.183	0.185	0.185	0.182	0.185	0.190	0.192	0.193	0.198	0.193	0.199	0.205
Dec.	0.187	0.190	0.190	0.186	0.189	0.194	0.196	0.198	0.202	0.197	0.203	0.210
1993 *Jan.*	0.198	0.201	0.201	0.197	0.200	0.205	0.207	0.209	0.213	0.208	0.215	0.221
Feb.	0.190	0.193	0.193	0.189	0.192	0.197	0.200	0.201	0.205	0.200	0.207	0.213
March	0.186	0.189	0.189	0.185	0.188	0.193	0.195	0.197	0.201	0.196	0.202	0.209
April	0.175	0.178	0.178	0.174	0.177	0.182	0.184	0.186	0.190	0.185	0.191	0.198
May	0.171	0.174	0.174	0.170	0.173	0.178	0.180	0.181	0.186	0.181	0.187	0.193
June	0.172	0.174	0.174	0.171	0.174	0.179	0.181	0.182	0.187	0.182	0.188	0.194
July	0.174	0.177	0.177	0.173	0.176	0.181	0.183	0.185	0.189	0.184	0.190	0.197
Aug.	0.169	0.172	0.172	0.168	0.171	0.176	0.178	0.180	0.184	0.179	0.185	0.192
Sept.	0.164	0.167	0.167	0.163	0.166	0.171	0.173	0.175	0.179	0.174	0.180	0.187
Oct.	0.165	0.168	0.168	0.164	0.167	0.172	0.174	0.176	0.180	0.175	0.181	0.188
Nov.	0.167	0.169	0.169	0.166	0.169	0.174	0.176	0.177	0.181	0.177	0.183	0.189
Dec.	0.164	0.167	0.167	0.163	0.166	0.171	0.173	0.175	0.179	0.174	0.180	0.187
1994 *Jan.*	0.169	0.172	0.172	0.168	0.171	0.176	0.178	0.180	0.184	0.179	0.185	0.192
Feb.	0.163	0.165	0.165	0.162	0.165	0.170	0.172	0.173	0.177	0.172	0.179	0.185

RD Month (April 1999–March 2000) January 1987 = 100

	1999 *April*	*May*	*June*	*July*	*Aug.*	*Sept.*	*Oct.*	*Nov.*	*Dec.*	2000 *Jan.*	*Feb.*	*Mar.*
RI Month												
1994 *March*	1.159	0.162	0.162	0.159	0.161	0.166	0.168	0.170	0.174	0.169	0.175	0.182
April	1.146	0.148	0.148	0.145	0.148	0.153	0.155	0.156	0.160	0.155	0.162	0.168
May	1.142	0.144	0.144	0.141	0.144	0.149	0.151	0.152	0.156	0.151	0.158	0.164
June	1.142	0.144	0.144	0.141	0.144	0.149	0.151	0.152	0.156	0.151	0.158	0.164
July	1.147	0.150	0.150	0.147	0.149	0.154	0.156	0.158	0.162	0.157	0.163	0.169
Aug.	1.142	0.144	0.144	0.141	0.144	0.149	0.151	0.152	0.156	0.151	0.158	0.164
Sept.	1.139	0.142	0.142	0.139	0.141	0.146	0.148	0.150	0.154	0.149	0.155	0.161
Oct.	1.138	0.140	0.140	0.137	0.140	0.145	0.147	0.148	0.152	0.147	0.154	0.160
Nov.	0.137	0.140	0.140	0.136	0.139	0.144	0.146	0.147	0.151	0.147	0.153	0.159
Dec.	0.132	0.134	0.134	0.131	0.134	0.138	0.140	0.142	0.146	0.141	0.147	0.153
1995 *Jan.*	0.132	0.134	0.134	0.131	0.134	0.138	0.140	0.142	0.146	0.141	0.147	0.153
Feb.	0.125	0.127	0.127	0.124	0.127	0.131	0.133	0.135	0.139	0.134	0.140	0.146
March	0.120	0.123	0.123	0.119	0.122	0.127	0.129	0.130	0.134	0.129	0.136	0.142
April	0.109	0.111	0.111	0.108	0.111	0.115	0.117	0.119	0.123	0.118	0.124	0.130
May	0.104	0.107	0.107	0.104	0.106	0.111	0.113	0.114	0.118	0.114	0.120	0.126
June	0.103	0.105	0.105	0.102	0.105	0.109	0.111	0.113	0.117	0.112	0.118	0.124
July	0.108	0.111	0.111	0.107	0.110	0.115	0.117	0.118	0.122	0.117	0.123	0.129
Aug.	0.102	0.105	0.105	0.101	0.104	0.109	0.111	0.112	0.116	0.111	0.117	0.123
Sept.	0.097	0.100	0.100	0.096	0.099	0.104	0.106	0.107	0.111	0.106	0.112	0.118
Oct.	0.103	0.105	0.105	0.102	0.105	0.109	0.111	0.113	0.117	0.112	0.118	0.124
Nov.	0.103	0.105	0.105	0.102	0.105	0.109	0.111	0.113	0.117	0.112	0.118	0.124
Dec.	0.096	0.099	0.099	0.096	0.098	0.103	0.105	0.106	0.110	0.106	0.111	0.117
1996 *Jan.*	0.100	0.103	0.103	0.099	0.102	0.107	0.109	0.110	0.114	0.109	0.115	0.121
Feb.	0.095	0.097	0.097	0.094	0.097	0.101	0.103	0.105	0.109	0.104	0.110	0.116
March	0.090	0.093	0.093	0.090	0.092	0.097	0.099	0.100	0.104	0.100	0.106	0.112
April	0.083	0.085	0.085	0.082	0.085	0.089	0.091	0.092	0.096	0.092	0.098	0.104
May	0.080	0.083	0.083	0.080	0.082	0.087	0.089	0.090	0.094	0.090	0.095	0.101
June	0.080	0.082	0.082	0.079	0.082	0.086	0.088	0.090	0.093	0.089	0.095	0.101
July	0.084	0.087	0.087	0.083	0.086	0.091	0.093	0.094	0.098	0.093	0.099	0.105
Aug.	0.079	0.082	0.082	0.078	0.081	0.086	0.088	0.089	0.093	0.088	0.094	0.100
Sept.	0.074	0.077	0.077	0.073	0.076	0.081	0.083	0.084	0.088	0.083	0.089	0.095
Oct.	0.074	0.077	0.077	0.073	0.076	0.081	0.083	0.084	0.088	0.083	0.089	0.095
Nov.	0.073	0.076	0.076	0.073	0.075	0.080	0.082	0.083	0.087	0.083	0.088	0.094
Dec.	0.070	0.073	0.073	0.069	0.072	0.076	0.078	0.080	0.084	0.079	0.085	0.091
1997 *Jan.*	0.070	0.073	0.073	0.069	0.072	0.076	0.078	0.080	0.084	0.079	0.085	0.091
Feb.	0.066	0.068	0.068	0.065	0.068	0.072	0.074	0.075	0.079	0.075	0.081	0.086

RD Month (April 1999–March 2000) January 1987 = 100

RI Month	1999 *April*	*May*	*June*	*July*	*Aug.*	*Sept.*	*Oct.*	*Nov.*	*Dec.*	2000 *Jan.*	*Feb.*	*Mar.*
1997 *March*	0.063	0.066	0.066	0.062	0.065	0.069	0.071	0.073	0.077	0.072	0.078	0.084
April	0.057	0.060	0.060	0.056	0.059	0.063	0.065	0.067	0.070	0.066	0.072	0.077
May	0.053	0.055	0.055	0.052	0.055	0.059	0.061	0.062	0.066	0.062	0.068	0.073
June	0.049	0.051	0.051	0.048	0.051	0.055	0.057	0.058	0.062	0.058	0.063	0.069
July	0.049	0.051	0.051	0.048	0.051	0.055	0.057	0.058	0.062	0.058	0.063	0.069
Aug.	0.042	0.045	0.045	0.042	0.044	0.049	0.050	0.052	0.056	0.051	0.057	0.062
Sept.	0.037	0.040	0.040	0.036	0.039	0.043	0.045	0.046	0.050	0.046	0.051	0.057
Oct.	0.036	0.038	0.038	0.035	0.038	0.042	0.044	0.045	0.049	0.045	0.050	0.056
Nov.	0.035	0.038	0.038	0.034	0.037	0.041	0.043	0.044	0.048	0.044	0.049	0.055
Dec.	0.032	0.035	0.035	0.032	0.034	0.039	0.041	0.042	0.046	0.041	0.047	0.053
1998 *Jan.*	0.036	0.038	0.038	0.035	0.038	0.042	0.044	0.045	0.049	0.045	0.050	0.056
Feb.	0.031	0.033	0.033	0.030	0.032	0.037	0.039	0.040	0.044	0.039	0.045	0.051
March	0.027	0.030	0.030	0.027	0.029	0.034	0.035	0.037	0.040	0.036	0.042	0.047
April	0.016	0.018	0.018	0.015	0.018	0.022	0.024	0.025	0.029	0.025	0.030	0.036
May	0.010	0.013	0.013	0.010	0.012	0.017	0.018	0.020	0.023	0.019	0.024	0.030
June	0.011	0.013	0.013	0.010	0.013	0.017	0.019	0.020	0.024	0.020	0.025	0.031
July	0.013	0.016	0.016	0.013	0.015	0.020	0.021	0.023	0.026	0.022	0.028	0.033
Aug.	0.009	0.012	0.012	0.009	0.011	0.015	0.017	0.018	0.022	0.018	0.023	0.029
Sept.	0.005	0.007	0.007	0.004	0.007	0.011	0.013	0.014	0.018	0.013	0.019	0.024
Oct.	0.004	0.007	0.007	0.004	0.006	0.010	0.012	0.013	0.017	0.013	0.018	0.024
Nov.	0.005	0.007	0.007	0.004	0.007	0.011	0.013	0.014	0.018	0.013	0.019	0.024
Dec.	0.005	0.007	0.004	0.004	0.007	0.011	0.013	0.014	0.018	0.013	0.019	0.024
1999 *Jan.*	0.011	0.013	0.013	0.010	0.013	0.017	0.019	0.020	0.024	0.020	0.025	0.031
Feb.	0.009	0.012	0.012	0.009	0.011	0.015	0.017	0.018	0.022	0.018	0.023	0.029
March	0.007	0.009	0.009	0.006	0.009	0.013	0.015	0.016	0.020	0.015	0.021	0.026
April	–	0.002	0.002	NIL	0.002	0.006	0.008	0.009	0.013	0.008	0.014	0.019
May		–	NIL	NIL	NIL	0.004	0.005	0.007	0.010	0.006	0.011	0.017
June			–	NIL	NIL	0.004	0.005	0.007	0.010	0.006	0.011	0.017
July				–	0.002	0.007	0.008	0.010	0.013	0.009	0.015	0.020
Aug.					–	0.004	0.006	0.007	0.011	0.007	0.012	0.018
Sept.						–	0.002	0.003	0.007	0.002	0.008	0.013
Oct.							–	0.001	0.005	0.001	0.006	0.011
Nov.								–	0.004	Nil	0.005	0.010
Dec.									–	Nil	0.001	0.007
2000 *Jan.*										–	0.005	0.011
Feb.											–	0.005
March												–

Taper relief (applies to individuals, trustees and personal representatives, NOT companies)

(TCGA 1992, s. 2A and Sch. A1)

Introduced for gains realised on or after 6 April 1998.

The chargeable gain is reduced according to how long the asset has been held or treated as held after 5 April 1998. For disposals on or before 5 April 2000, all assets acquired prior to 17 March 1998 qualify for an addition of one year to the period for which they are treated as held after 5 April 1998. For disposals on or after 6 April 2000, only non-business assets qualify for the additional year.

The taper is applied to the net chargeable gain for the year after deduction of any losses of the same tax year and of any losses carried forward from earlier years.

The relief is more generous for business assets, defined as:

- an asset used for the purposes of a trade caried on by the individual;
- an asset held for the purposes of a qualifying office or employment; or
- qualifying shareholding in a 'qualifying' company.

A 'qualifying' company is a trading company (or holding company of a trading group). On or before 5 April 2000, a qualifying shareholding is one in which the individual holds shares in a qualifying company which entitle that individual to exercise at least:

- 5 per cent of the voting rights and the individual is a full-time working officer or full-time employee of that company; or
- 25 per cent of the voting rights.

On or after 6 April 2000, a qualifying shareholding comprises:

- all shareholdings held by employees or officers (full time and part-time) in unquoted or quoted trading companies;
- shareholdings in a quoted trading company where the holder is not an officer or employer but who can exercise at least 5 per cent of the voting rights.

Where shares qualify as a business asset only from 6 April 2000, an apportionment of the eventual gain is necessary so that part qualifies for business taper and the balance for non-business taper.

Gains on business assets			**Gains on non-business assets**		
Number of *complete* years after 5.4.98 for which asset held	**Percentage of gain chargeable**	**Equivalent tax rates**	**Number of *complete* years after 5.4.98 for which asset held**	**Percentage of gain chargeable**	**Equivalent tax rates**
0	100	40/20/10	0	100	40/20/10
1	87.5	35/17.5/8.75	1	100	40/20/10
2	75	30/15/7.5	2	100	40/20/10
3	50	20/10/5	3	95	38/21.85
4 or more	25	10/5/2.5	4	90	36/20.70
			5	85	34/19.55
			6	80	32/18.40
			7	75	30/17.25
			8	70	28/16.10
			9	65	26/14.95
			10 or more	60	24/13.80

trt trt97b Mp 88—trt 120

For disposals of business assets arising in the period from 6 April 1998 to 5 April 2000, the following table applies:

Gains on business assets	
Number of *complete* years after 5.4.98 for which asset held	**Percentage of gain chargeable**
0	100
1	92.5
2	85
3	77.5

Note
For disposals on or after 6 April 2000, capital gains may be chargeable to capital gains tax at 40%, 20% or 10% depending on the level of total income.

Treatment of shares and other securities (after 5 April 1998)

(TCGA 1992, s. 106A)

Pooling for capital gains tax (but not corporation tax) ceased for acquisitions on or after 6 April 1998.

Disposals after 5 April 1998 are identified with acquisitions in the following order:

1. same day acquisitions (under existing rule);
2. acquisitions within following 30 days;
3. previous acquisitions after 5 April 1998 on LIFO (Last-In-First-Out) basis;
4. any shares in 'pool' at 5 April 1998;
5. any shares held at 5 April 1982; and
6. any shares acquired before 6 April 1965.

If the above identification rules fail to exhaust the shares disposed of, they are identified with subsequent acquisitions.

Enterprise Investment Scheme

(TCGA 1992, s. 150A & Sch. 5B)

Under the Enterprise Investment Scheme (EIS), income tax relief, CGT deferral relief and CGT disposal relief may be available and claimed. The income tax relief is based on the amount subscribed by a qualifying individual for eligible shares in a qualifying company. Income tax relief may be withdrawn under certain circumstances. With regards to the CGT reliefs:

(1) CGT Deferral Relief – Gains arising on the disposal of any asset can be deferred against subscriptions made by a qualifying individual for eligible shares in a qualifying company. For shares issued on or after 6 April 1998, shares no longer have to have EIS Income Tax Relief attributable to them in order to qualify for CGT Deferral Relief. The deferred gains may crystallise on the disposal of the shares.

(2) CGT Disposal Relief – Gains arising on the disposal by a qualifying individual of eligible shares in a qualifying company are exempt from CGT provided the shares have been held for a minimum period or the EIS Income Tax Relief has not been withdrawn.

'Qualifying individual' is basically someone who is not connected with the qualifying company.
'Eligible shares' are basically ordinary unquoted shares in a company.
'Qualifying company' is basically an unquoted company existing wholly for the purposes of carrying on a 'qualifying trade', or whose business consists entirely in the holding of shares in, or the making of loans to, one or more 'qualifying subsidiaries'.
'Qualifying trade' is basically one that is conducted on a commercial basis with a view to realising profits other than specifically excluded activities.
'Qualifying subsidiary' is basically one carrying on a qualifying trade.

Roll-over relief

(TCGA 1992, s. 155)

To qualify for roll-over or hold-over relief on the replacement of business assets, the items must be appropriate business assets (see below) and the reinvestment must generally take place within 12 months before, or three years after, the disposal of the old asset. For hold-over relief, the replacement asset is a depreciating asset (an asset with a predictable useful life of no more than 60 years).

Classes of assets qualifying for relief:

- land and buildings occupied and used exclusively for the purposes of a trade;
- fixed plant or fixed machinery;
- ships, aircraft, hovercraft;
- satellites, space stations and spacecraft (including launch vehicles);
- goodwill;
- milk quotas, potato quotas and fish quotas; and
- ewe and suckler cow premium quotas.

Retirement relief

(TCGA 1992, s. 163–164 and Sch. 6)

Retirement relief exempts from CGT a certain proportion of the gain from the disposal of a business by an individual who is aged 50 or over, or who retires earlier due to ill health.

It is phased out from 6 April 1999 by a gradual reduction of the relief thresholds and will cease to be available from 6 April 2003.

The annual thresholds are as follows:

Year	100% relief on gains up to: £	50% relief on gains between: £
1993–94 (to 28.11.93)	150,000	150,000–600,000
1993–94 (from 29.11.93)	250,000	250,000–1,000,000
1994–95 to 1998–99	250,000	250,001–1,000,000
1999–2000	200,000	200,001–800,000
2000-01	150,000	150,001–600,000
2001-02	100,000	100,001–400,000
2002-03	50,000	50,001–200,000

Charities

(TCGA 1992, s. 256(1))

The gains of charities are not taxable provided they are applicable, and applied, for charitable purposes only. Provisions contained in ICTA 1988, s. 505, 506 are designed to charge charities to tax on the amount of their income and gains that has not been invested, lent or spent in an approved way.

A charge to capital gains tax arises if a charity ceases to be a charity, when there is a deemed sale and reacquisition of the trust property by the trustees at market value.

Expenses incurred by personal representatives

(SP 8/94)

In respect of deaths after 5 April 1993, the scale of expenses allowable in computing the gains or losses of personal representatives on the sale of assets in a deceased person's estate is as follows:

Gross value of estate	Allowable expenditure
Up to £40,000	1.75% of probate value of assets sold by personal representatives
£40,001–£70,000	£700, divided among all assets in the estate in proportion to their probate values and allowed in those proportions on assets sold by personal representatives
£70,001–£300,000	1% of probate value of assets sold
£300,001–£400,000	£3,000, divided as above
£400,001–£750,000	0.75% of probate value of assets sold
Over £750,000	Negotiated with the inspector

Note
Computations based either on the above scale or on actual expenditure incurred are accepted.

Time-limits for elections and claims

In the absence of any provision to the contrary, under self-assessment the normal rule is that claims are to be made within five years from 31 January next following the tax year to which they relate, otherwise the limit is six years from the end of the relevant chargeable period (TMA 1970, s. 43(1)).

For details of time-limits relating to payment of tax, see pp. 10, 47, 80 and 94.

In certain cases the Board *may* permit an extension of the strict time-limit in relation to certain elections and claims.

Provision	Time-limit	Statutory reference
Post-cessation expenses relieved against gains	12 months from 31 January next following the tax year in which expenses paid	ICTA 1988, s. 109A
Trading losses relieved against gains	12 months from 31 January next following the tax year loss arose	ICTA 1988, s. 380; FA 1991, s. 72
Value of asset negligible	2 years from end of tax year (or accounting period if a company) in which deemed disposal/ reacquisition takes place	TCGA 1992, s. 24(2)
Re-basing of all assets to 31 March 1982 values	Within 12 months from 31 January next following the tax year of disposal (or 2 years from end of accounting period of disposal if a company)	TCGA 1992, s. 35(6)
50% relief if deferred charge on gains before 31 March 1982	Within 12 months from 31 January next following the tax year of disposal (or 2 years from end of accountancy period of disposal if a company)	TCGA 1992, s. 36 and Sch. 4, para. 9(1)
Variation within 2 years of death not to have CGT effect	6 months from date of variation	TCGA 1992, s. 62(7)
Replacement of business assets (roll-over relief)	5 years from 31 January next following the tax year (or 6 years from the end of the accounting period if a company) Replacement asset to be purchased between 12 months before and 3 years after disposal of old asset	TCGA 1992, s. 152(1)
Disposal of asset and re-investment in qualifying company (prior to 30 November 1993, applied only to disposal of qualifying shares or securities) (re-investment relief)	5 years from 31 January next following the tax year	TCGA 1992, 164A(2)
Hold-over of gain on gift of business asset	5 years from 31 January next following the tax year	TCGA 1992, s. 165(1)
Determination of main residence	2 years from acquisition of second property (see ESC D21)	TCGA 1992, s. 222(5)
Irrecoverable loan to a trader	2 years from end of tax year (or accounting period if a company) otherwise effective from date claimed (see ESC D38, SP 8/90)	TCGA 1992, s. 253(3)
Retirement relief: ill-health grounds	12 months from 31 January next following the year of assessment in which the disposal occurred	TCGA 1992, Sch. 6, para. 5(2)

INHERITANCE TAX

Rates 10 March 1992 to 2000–2001

(IHTA 1984, s. 7, Sch. 1)

Gross cumulative total £	Gross rate of tax %	Tax on band £	Cumulative tax payable £	Net cumulative total £	Tax on each £ *over* net cumulative total for grossing up
Lifetime transfers					
After 5 April 2000					
234,000	Nil	Nil	Nil	234,000	1/4
Over 234,000	20	—	—	—	—
6 April 1999–5 April 2000					
231,000	Nil	Nil	Nil	231,000	1/4
Over 231,000	20	—	—	—	—
6 April 1998–5 April 1999					
223,000	Nil	Nil	Nil	223,000	1/4
Over 223,000	20	—	—	—	—
6 April 1997–5 April 1998					
215,000	Nil	Nil	Nil	215,000	1/4
Over 215,000	20	—	—	—	—
6 April 1996–5 April 1997					
200,000	Nil	Nil	Nil	200,000	1/4
Over 200,000	20	—	—	—	—
6 April 1995–5 April 1996					
154,000	Nil	Nil	Nil	154,000	1/4
Over 154,000	20	—	—	—	—
10 March 1992–5 April 1995					
150,000	Nil	Nil	Nil	150,000	1/4
Over 150,000	20	—	—	—	—
Transfers on death					
After 5 April 2000					
234,000	Nil	Nil	Nil	234,000	2/3
Over 234,000	40	—	—	—	—
6 April 1999–5 April 2000					
231,000	Nil	Nil	Nil	231,000	2/3
Over 231,000	40	—	—	—	—
6 April 1998–5 April 1999					
223,000	Nil	Nil	Nil	223,000	2/3
Over 223,000	40	—	—	—	—
6 April 1997–5 April 1998					
215,000	Nil	Nil	Nil	215,000	2/3
Over 215,000	40	—	—	—	—
6 April 1996-5 April 1997					
200,000	Nil	Nil	Nil	200,000	2/3
Over 200,000	40	—	—	—	—
6 April 1995–5 April 1996					
154,000	Nil	Nil	Nil	154,000	2/3
Over 154,000	40	—	—	—	—
10 March 1992–5 April 1995					
150,000	Nil	Nil	Nil	150,000	2/3
Over 150,000	40	—	—	—	—

Note

The above scales apply to lifetime transfers made within seven years before death. For the tapered reduction in tax payable on transfers made between seven and three years before death, see following.

trt trt97b Mp 93—trt 140

Taper relief

(IHTA 1984, s. 7(4))

Years between gift and death		Percentage of full tax charge at death rates actually due
More than	Not more than	
3	4	80
4	5	60
5	6	40
6	7	20

Prescribed rates of interest

(IHTA 1984, s. 233)

Period of application	Rate %
From 6 February 2000	5
6 March 1999 to 5 February 2000	4
6 October 1994 to 5 March 1999	5
6 January 1994 to 5 October 1994	4

Due dates for payment

(IHTA 1984, s. 226)

Transfer	Due date
Chargeable lifetime transfers between 6 April and 30 September	30 April in following year
Chargeable lifetime transfers between 1 October and 5 April	Six months after end of month in which transfer made
Potentially exempt transfers which become chargeable	Six months after end of month in which death occurred
Transfers on death; extra tax payable on chargeable lifetime transfers within seven years before death	Six months after end of month in which death occurred

Reliefs

Type of relief	Rate of relief for disposals			
	Before 10/3/92	10/3/92–31/8/95	1/9/95–5/4/96	On or after 6/4/96
Agricultural property (IHTA 1984, s. 115ff.)[1] Vacant possession or right to obtain it within 12 months	% 50	% 100	% 100	% 100
Tenanted land with a vacant possession value	50	100	100	100
Entitled to 50% relief at 9 March 1981 and not since able to obtain vacant possession	50	100	100	100
Agricultural land let on or after 1 September 1995	N/A	N/A	100	100
Other circumstances	30	50	50	50
Business property (IHTA 1984, s. 103ff.) *Nature of property* Business or interest in business	50	100	100	100
Controlling shareholding in quoted company	50	50	50	50
Controlling shareholding in unquoted[2] company	50	100	100	100
Settled property used in life tenant's business	50/30[3]	100/50[3]	100/50[3]	100/50[3]
Shareholding in unquoted[2] company: more than 25% interest	50[4]	100	100	100
Minority shareholding in unquoted[2] company: 25% or less	30[5]	50	50	100
Land, buildings, machinery or plant used by transferor's company or partnership	30	50	50	50

Notes

[1] From 6 April 1995, short rotation coppice is regarded as agricultural property.

[2] With effect from 10 March 1992, 'unquoted' means shares not quoted on a recognised stock exchange and therefore includes shares dealt in on the Unlisted Securities Market (USM) or Alternative Investment Market (AIM).

[3] The higher rate applies if the settled property is transferred along with the business itself (*Fetherstonhaugh & Ors v IR Commrs* [1984] BTC 8,046).

[4] 30% if a minority interest transferred before 17 March 1987, or if transferor had not held at least 25% interest throughout preceding two years.

[5] The relief was 20% for transfers after 26 October 1977 but before 15 March 1983.

Quick succession relief
(IHTA 1984, s. 141)

Years between transfers		Percentage applied to formula below
More than	Not more than	
0	1	100
1	2	80
2	3	60
3	4	40
4	5	20

Formula

$$\text{Tax charge on earlier transfer} \times \frac{\text{Increase in transferee's estate}}{\text{Diminution in transferor's estate}}$$

Instalment option
(IHTA 1984, s. 227ff.)

Interest-free
- Controlling shareholdings
- Holdings of 10% or more of unquoted shares with value over £20,000
- Certain other death transfers of unquoted shares
- Business or interest in a business
- Agricultural value of agricultural property
- Woodlands

Not interest-free
- Land, wherever situated, other than within the categories above
- Shareholdings in certain land, investment and security dealing companies or market makers or discount houses

Exemptions

Annual and small gift exemption
(IHTA 1984, s. 19, 20)

	On or after 6 April 1981 £
Annual	3,000
Small gift	250

Gifts in consideration of marriage
(IHTA 1984, s. 22)

Identity of donor	Exemption limit £
Parent of party to marriage	5,000
Remoter ancestor of party to marriage	2,500
Party to marriage	2,500
Any other person	1,000

Gift by UK-domiciled spouse to non UK-domiciled spouse
(IHTA 1984, s. 18)

Transfer on or after	Exemption limit £
9 March 1982	55,000

Delivery of accounts

(IHTA 1984, s. 216)

Transaction	Time limit
Chargeable lifetime transfer	Later of: • 12 months after end of month in which transfer occurred • 3 months after person became liable
Potentially exempt transfers which have become chargeable	12 months after end of month in which death of transferor occurred
Transfers on death	Later of: • 12 months after end of month in which death occurred • 3 months after personal representatives first act or have reason to believe an account is required
Gifts subject to reservation included in donor's estate at death	12 months after end of month in which death occurred
National heritage property	6 months after end of month in which chargeable event occurred

Penalties for failure in relation to obligations falling due after 26 July 1999

Failure to deliver an IHT account (IHTA 1984, s. 216)	Account outstanding at end of statutory period	Up to £100 (but not exceeding tax due)
	Daily penalty after failure declared by a court or the Special Commissioners	Up to £60 a day
	Further penalty after six months from end of statutory period, if proceedings for declaring the failure not started before then	Up to £100 (but not exceeding tax due)
Failure by professional person to deliver a return of a settlement by a UK domiciled person but with non-resident trustees (IHTA 1984, s. 218)	Account outstanding at end of statutory period (three months from making of settlement)	Up to £300
	Daily penalty after failure declared by a court or the Special Commissioners	Up to £60 a day
Failure to comply with a notice requiring information (IHTA 1984, s. 219)	Penalty	Up to £300
	Daily penalty after failure declared by a court or the Special Commissioners	Up to £60 a day
Failure to comply with a notice requiring documents, accounts or particulars (IHTA 1984, s. 219A)	Penalty	Up to £50
	Daily penalty after failure declared by a court or the Special Commissioners	Up to £30 a day
Incorrect information provided by persons liable to tax (IHTA 1984, s. 247)	Fraud	Up to £3,000 plus the amount of the extra tax
	Negligence	Up to £1,500 plus the amount of the extra tax
Incorrect information provided by others (IHTA 1984, s. 247)	Fraud	Up to £3,000
	Negligence	Up to £1,500
Person assisting in providing incorrect information etc (IHTA 1984, s. 247)	Penalty	Up to £3,000

Values below which no account required

(IHTA 1984, s. 256; SI 1981/880, 881, 1440 and 1441 as amended)

Excepted lifetime chargeable transfers on and after 1 April 1981	**£**
Transfer in question, together with all other chargeable transfers in same 12-month period ending on 5 April	10,000
Transfer in question, together with all previous chargeable transfers during preceding ten years	40,000

Excepted estates

Deaths on and after	**But before**	**Total gross value[1] £**	**Total gross value of property outside UK £**	**Aggregate value of 'specified transfers' £**
6 April 2000		210,000	50,000	75,000
6 April 1998	5 April 2000	200,000	50,000	75,000
6 April 1996	5 April 1998	180,000	30,000	50,000
6 April 1995	6 April 1996	145,000	15,000	
1 April 1991	6 April 1995	125,000	15,000	

Note

[1] For deaths on or after 6 April 1996 this limit applies to the total gross value of the estate *plus* the value of any transfers of cash or of quoted shares or securities made within seven years before death.

STAMP DUTIES

Conveyance or transfer on sale of shares and securities

Instrument	Rate of tax after 26 October 1986 ('Big Bang') %	Previous rates	
		From 25 March 1986 to 26 October 1986 %	From 20 March 1984 to 24 March 1986 %
Stock transfer	$\frac{1}{2}$	1	1
Conversion of shares into depositary receipts	$1\frac{1}{2}$	$1\frac{1}{2}$	1
Take overs and mergers	$\frac{1}{2}$	$\frac{1}{2}$	Nil
Purchase by company of own shares Letters of allotment	$\frac{1}{2}$	Nil	Nil

Other conveyance or transfer on sale (e.g. conveyance or transfer of freehold property)

Instruments executed	Thresholds			
	Up to £60,000	Over £60,000 up to £250,000	Over £250,000 up to £500,000	Over £500,000
On or after 28 March 2000[1]	Nil	1%	3%	4%
On or after 16 March 1999[2]	Nil	1%	2.5%	3.5%
On or after 24 March 1998[3]	Nil	1%	2%	3%
On or after 8 July 1997[4]	Nil	1%	$1\frac{1}{2}$%	2%
On or after 16 March 1993[5]	Nil	1%	1%	1%

Notes

[1] Transfers executed on or after 28 March 2000 unless in pursuance of a contract made on or before 21 March 2000.
[2] Transfers executed on or after 16 March 1999 unless in pursuance of a contract made on or before 9 March 1999.
[3] Transfers executed on or after 24 March 1998 unless in pursuance of a contract made on or before 17 March 1998.
[4] Transfers executed on or after 8 July 1997 unless in pursuance of a contract made on or before 2 July 1997.
[5] If stamped on or after 23 March 1993.

Stamp duty at the appropriate rate is charged on the *full* amount of the certified value, not just on any excess over a threshold.

Fixed duties

In relation to instruments executed on or after 1 October 1999, the amount of fixed stamp duty is £5 (FA 1999, s. 112[2]). The earlier amounts of fixed duties are as follows:

Duty	Amount
Conveyance or transfer – miscellaneous	50p
Declaration of trust	50p
Duplicate or counterpart	50p
Exchange or partition	50p
Leases – small furnished letting	£1
– miscellaneous	£2
Release or renunciation	50p
Surrender	50p

Leases

Rates for instruments executed after 27 March 2000

Term (FA 1999, Sch. 13, para. 12(3))	Rate %
Under 7 years or indefinite:	
• rent £5,000 or less	Nil
• over £5,000	1
Over 7 but not over 35 years	2
Over 35 but not over 100 years	12
Over 100 years	24

Notes

[1] Leases for a definite term of less than one year: fixed duty of £5 (FA 1999, Sch. 13, para. 11 with effect from 1 October 1999).

[2] Where a furnished property lease is granted for a premium, this will be subject to stamp duty as set out in the table on p. 96 with the nil rate only applying if the annual rent does not exceed:

- £600 per annum for documents executed on or after 16 March 1993 and stamped on or after 23 March 1993;
- £300 per annum for documents executed before 16 March 1993.

[3] In the table above, the £5,000 limit was £500 in the period from 1 October 1999 to 27 March 2000 inclusive.

Agreements for lease

An agreement for lease is liable to stamp duty as if it were an actual lease, but if a lease is subsequently granted which is in conformity with the agreement, or which relates to substantially the same property and term of years as the agreement, the duty on the lease is reduced by the duty already paid on the agreement.

Interest on repaid and overdue stamp duty

In respect of instruments executed on or after 1 October 1999, interest is chargeable on stamp duty that is not paid within 30 days of execution of a stampable document, wherever execution takes place (*Stamp Act* 1891, s. 15A). Interest is rounded down (if necessary) to the nearest multiple of £5. No interest is payable if that amount is under £25. The applicable interest rate is as prescribed under FA 1989, s. 178.

Penalty for late stamping

A penalty can be imposed if an instrument is not presented for stamping within 30 days after execution (or where executed outside the UK, the day on which it was first received in the UK).

The penalty is the greater of £300 or the amount of the unpaid duty if the instrument is presented more than one year after the end of the 30-day period (*Stamp Act* 1891, s. 15B).

Stamp duty reserve tax

Principal charge (FA 1986, s. 87)

Subject matter of charge	Rate of tax %
Agreements to transfer chargeable securities[1] for money or money's worth	0.5
Renounceable letters of allotment	0.5
Shares converted into depositary receipts	1.5
but transfer of shares or securities on which stamp duty payable	1
Shares put into clearance system	1.5
but transfer of shares or securities on which stamp duty payable	1

Note

[1] Chargeable securities = stocks, shares, loan capital units under unit trust scheme (FA 1986, s. 99(3)).

Interest on repaid and overdue stamp duty reserve tax (SDRT)

SDRT carries interest as follows:

- interest is charged on SDRT paid late (TMA 1970, s. 86 via SI 1986/1711, reg. 13);
- repayment of SDRT carry interest from the date that SDRT was paid (FA 1989, s. 178 via SI 1986/1711, reg. 11); and
- similarly, SDRT is repaid with interest if an instrument is duly stamped within six years of the date of the agreement (FA 1986, s. 92).

For interest periods from 1 October 1999 onwards, the rate of interest charged on underpaid or late paid SDRT exceeds that on SDRT repayments:

Period of application	Rate %	
	Underpayments	Repayments
From 6 February 2000	8.50	4.00
1 October 1999 to 5 February 2000	7.50	3.00

For interest periods up to 1 October 1999, these were all at the same rate:

Period of application		Rate %
6 March 1999 to	30 September 1999	5.75
6 January 1999 to	5 March 1999	6.50
6 August 1997 to	5 January 1999	7.25
6 February 1996 to	5 August 1997	6.25
6 March 1995 to	5 February 1996	7.00
6 October 1994 to	5 March 1995	6.25
6 January 1994 to	5 October 1994	5.50
6 March 1993 to	5 January 1994	6.25

Penalty for late presentation of documents for stamping

Documents executed on or after 1 October 1999 (SA 1891, s. 15B)

Penalties apply if documents are presented for stamping more than 30 days after, either execution in the UK, or being first received in the UK, if executed abroad. Written confirmation will be required of the date a document is brought into the UK (thereby introducing the possibility of a free standing penalty if this information is incorrect; see below). The maximum penalties are:

- £300 or the amount of duty, whichever is less; on documents submitted up to one year late; and
- £300 or the amount of duty, whichever is greater; on documents submitted more than one year late.

The Stamp Office publishes tables (booklet SO10) of mitigated penalty levels that will be applied in straightforward cases.

Mitigated penalties due on late stamping:

Cases involving *ad valorem* duties

Months late	Up to £300	£300–£700	£705–£1,350	£1,355–£2,500	£2,505–£5,000	Over £5,000
Under 3	Nil	£20	£40	£60	£80	£100
Under 6	£20*	£40	£60	£80	£100	£150
Under 9	£40*	£60	£80	£100	£150	£200
Under 12	£60*	£80	£100	£150	£200	£300
Under 15	15% of the duty or £100 if greater					
Under 18	25% of the duty or £150 if greater					
Under 21	35% of the duty or £200 if greater					
Under 24	45% of the duty or £250 if greater					

Note
* Or the amount of the duty if that is less.

Cases over one year late involving duty over £5,000 and any case over two years late are considered individually.

Cases involving fixed duties

	Maximum penalty per document	Penalty after mitigation
Up to 12 months late	£5	Nil (100% mitigation)
Over 12 months late	£300	According to circumstances

In all cases above the penalties will not apply if the person responsible for stamping can show a "reasonable excuse" for the failure to submit the document(s) within the time limit. Interest is due on any unpaid penalty.

Free standing penalties (maximum amount)

- fraud in relation to Stamp Duty; (£3,000)
- failure to set out true facts, relating to stamp duty liability, in a document; (£3,000)
- failure to stamp document within 30 days of issue of a Notice of Decision on Adjudication; (£300)
- failure to allow inspection of documents; (£300)

- registering or enrolling a chargeable document that is not duly stamped; (£300)
- circulating a blank transfer; (£300)
- issuing an unstamped foreign security. (£300)

Documents executed prior to 1 October 1999 (old SA 1891, s. 15)

A penalty may be imposed where documents are stamped more than 30 days after, either execution in the UK, or being first received in the UK, if executed abroad. The penalties are either:

- £10; or
- where the unpaid duty exceeds £10; £10 *plus* interest on the unpaid duty at 5% per annum from the date of execution to the date that the accrued interest equals the unpaid duty.

Where ad valorem duties are due further penalties of £10 plus an amount equal to unpaid duty may be charged. The penalties will not apply if the person responsible for stamping can show a "reasonable excuse" for the failure to submit the document(s) within the time limit.

Duties abolished since March 1985

Duty	Effective date of abolition
Ad valorem	
• Capital duty	Transactions after 15 March 1988 – documents stamped after 21 March 1988
• Gifts inter vivos	Instruments executed after 18 March 1985, stamped after 25 March 1985
• Life assurance policy duty	Instruments executed after 31 December 1989
• Transfers on divorce etc.	Instruments executed after 25 March 1985
• Unit trust instrument duty	Instruments executed after 15 March 1988, stamped after 21 March 1988
• Variations and appropriations on death	Instruments executed after 25 March 1985
• Duty on Northern Ireland bank notes etc.	1 January 1992
• Transfers of intellectual property	Instruments executed after 27 March 2000
• Transfers to Registered Social Landlords	[Royal Assent to FA 2000]
Fixed duties	
• Agreement or contract made or entered into pursuant to the Highways Act. Appointment of a new trustee, and appointment in execution of a power of any property. Covenant. Deed of any kind whatsoever, not liable to other duties. Letter or power of attorney. Procuration. Revocation of any use or trust of any property by any writing, not being a will. Warrant of attorney. Letter of allotment and letter of renunciation. Scrip certificate, scrip.	Instruments executed after 25 March 1985
• Categories within the *Stamp Duty (Exempt Instruments) Regulations* 1987 (SI 1987/516):	Instruments executed after 30 April 1987
A. Trust vesting instrument	
B. Transfer of bequeathed property to legatee	
C. Transfer of intestate property to person entitled	
D. Certain appropriations on death	
E. Transfer to beneficiary of entitlement to residue	
F. Certain transfers to beneficiaries entitled under settlements	
G. Certain transfers in consideration of marriage	
H. Transfers in connection with divorce	
I. Transfers by liquidator to shareholder	
J. Grant of easement for no consideration	
K. Grant of servitude for no consideration	
L. Conveyance as voluntary disposition for no consideration	
M. Variations on death	
N. Declaration of trust of life policy	Instruments executed after 30 September 1999

Prospective abolitions

Duty	Effective date of abolition
All duties (including stamp duty reserve tax) except those duties on land and buildings described in FA 1991, s. 110	The 'abolition day' appointed by virtue of FA 1990, s. 111(1)[(1)].

Note

[(1)] The abolition day was to have broadly coincided with the implementation of the TAURUS system (London Stock Exchange News Release 40/91, 17 October 1991). However, on 11 March 1993 it was announced that TAURUS had been abandoned (London Stock Exchange News Release 6/93).

VALUE ADDED TAX

Rates

Period of application	Standard rate %	VAT fraction	Higher rate %	VAT fraction	Reduced rate %[1]	VAT fraction
From 1/4/94	$17^1/_2$	$^7/_{47}$	N/A	N/A	5	$^1/_{21}$
1/4/91–31/3/94	$17^1/_2$	$^7/_{47}$	N/A	N/A	N/A	N/A
18/6/79–31/3/91	15	$^3/_{23}$	N/A	N/A	N/A	N/A
12/4/76–17/6/79	8	$^2/_{27}$	$12^1/_2$	$^1/_9$	N/A	N/A
1/5/75–11/4/76	8	$^2/_{27}$	25[2]	$^1/_5$	N/A	N/A

Notes

[1] Supplies of fuel and power for domestic, residential and charity non-business use are charged at the reduced rate of 5% with effect from 1 September 1997 (8% from 1 April 1994 to 31 August 1997).
Supplies of energy-saving materials in connection with certain government grant schemes are charged at 5%.

[2] Re petrol, electrical appliances and luxury goods.

[3] Imports of certain works of art, antiques and collectors' items are charged at an effective rate of 5% from 27 July 1999 ($2^1/_2$% from 1 May 1995 to 26 July 1999).

Registration limits

Taxable supplies

Period of application	Past turnover (£)[1]		Future turnover (£)[1]
	1 year	Unless turnover for next year will not exceed	30 days[2]
From 1/4/2000	52,000	50,000	52,000
1/4/99–31/3/2000	51,000	49,000	51,000
1/4/98–31/3/99	50,000	48,000	50,000
1/12/97–31/3/98	49,000	47,000	49,000
27/11/96–30/11/97	48,000	46,000	48,000
29/11/95–26/11/96	47,000	45,000	47,000
30/11/94–28/11/95	46,000	44,000	46,000
1/12/93–29/11/94	45,000	43,000	45,000

Notes

[1] Value of taxable supplies at the zero rate and all positive rates are included.

[2] A person is liable to register if there are reasonable grounds for believing that the value of his taxable supplies in the period of 30 days then beginning will exceed this limit.

Supplies from other member states – distance selling

Period of application	Cumulative relevant supplies from 1 January in year to any day in same year £
From 1/1/93	exceed 70,000

(VATA 1994, Sch. 2; Leaflet 700/1A)

If certain goods subject to excise duty are removed to the UK, the person who removes the goods is liable to register in the UK because all such goods must be taxed in the country of destination. There is no de minimis limit.

Acquisitions from other member states

Period of application	Cumulative relevant acquisitions from 1 January in year to end of any month in same year £
From 1/4/2000	52,000
1/4/99–31/3/2000	51,000
1/4/98–31/3/99	50,000
1/1/98–31/3/98	49,000
1/1/97–31/12/97	48,000
1/1/96–31/12/96	47,000
1/1/95–31/12/95	46,000
1/1/94–31/12/94	45,000

Future prospects rule: a person is also liable to register at any time if there are reasonable grounds for believing that the value of his relevant acquisitions in the period of 30 days then beginning will exceed (from 1 April 2000) £52,000 (VATA 1994, Sch. 3; Leaflet 700/1B).

Assets supplied in the UK by overseas persons

From 21 March 2000, any person without an establishment in the UK making or intending to make 'relevant' supplies must VAT register, regardless of the value of those supplies (VATA 1994, Sch. 3A). 'Relevant' supplies are taxable supplies of goods, including capital assets, in the UK where the supplier has recovered UK VAT under the eighth or thirteenth VAT directive. This applies where:

(1) the supplier (or his predecessor in business) was charged VAT on the purchase of the goods, or on anything incorporated in them, and has either claimed it back or intends to do so; or

(2) the VAT being claimed back was VAT paid on the import of goods into the UK.

De-registration limits

Taxable supplies

Period of application	Future turnover £	Period of application	Future turnover £
From 1/4/2000	50,000	27/11/96–30/11/97	46,000
1/4/99–31/3/2000	49,000	29/11/95–26/11/96	45,000
1/4/98–31/3/99	48,000	30/11/94–28/11/95	44,000
1/12/97–31/3/98	47,000	1/12/93–29/11/94	43,000

Taxable supplies at both the zero rate and all positive rates are included in the above limits. However, the value of supplies of (1) 'capital assets' other than certain land supplies, (2) any taxable supplies which would not be taxable supplies apart from VATA 1994, s. 7(4), which concerns certain removals of goods to the UK, is excluded and (3) removals from a fiscal warehouse (VATA 1994, Sch. 1, para. 1 and 4; Leaflet 700/11).

Supplies from other member states

Period of application	Past relevant supplies in last year to 31 December £	Future relevant supplies in immediately following year £
From 1/1/93	70,000	70,000

Acquisitions from other member states

Period of application	Past relevant acquisitions in last year to 31 December £	Future relevant acquisitions in immediately following year £
From 1/4/2000	52,000	52,000
1/4/99–31/3/2000	51,000	51,000
1/4/98–31/3/99	50,000	50,000
1/1/98–31/3/98	49,000	49,000
1/1/97–31/12/97	48,000	48,000
1/1/96–31/12/96	47,000	47,000
1/1/95–31/12/95	46,000	46,000
1/1/94–31/12/94	45,000	45,000

Cash accounting: admission to the scheme

Period of application	Annual turnover[1] £
From 1/4/93	350,000
1/10/90–31/3/93	300,000
1/10/87–30/9/90	250,000

Notes

[1] Includes zero-rated supplies, but excludes any capital assets previously used in the business. Exempt supplies are also excluded.

[2] A person must withdraw from the cash accounting scheme at the end of a prescribed accounting period if the value of his taxable supplies in the one year ending at the end of the prescribed accounting period has exceeded £437,500 (*Value Added Tax Regulations* 1995 (SI 1995/2518), Pt. VIII).

Zero-rated supplies

(VATA 1994, Sch. 8)

Group
1. Food (this includes most food for human and animal consumption. The exceptions are mainly food supplied in the course of catering, confectionery, pet foods and hot take-away food)
2. Sewerage services and water (except distilled and bottled water) but not if supplied to industry
3. Books, pamphlets, newspapers, journals, maps, music etc. (but not stationery and posters)
4. Talking books for the blind and handicapped and wireless sets for the blind
5. Construction of buildings etc.
6. Protected buildings
7. International services
8. Transport
9. Caravans and houseboats
10. Gold
11. Bank notes
12. Drugs, medicines, aids for the handicapped etc.
13. Imports, exports etc.
14. Tax-free shops (repealed for supplies made after 30 June 1999)
15. Charities etc.
16. Clothing and footwear
Notes Except for exported goods and certain transactions in commodities, a supply is generally not zero-rated *unless* it is included in the zero-rated schedule (VATA 1994, Sch. 8). A supply which can be classified as zero-rated overrides exemption. A supply which is not outside the scope of VAT is standard-rated *unless* it falls within one of the categories of exempt or zero-rated or reduced-rated supplies.

Exempt supplies

(VATA 1994, Sch. 9)

Group
1. Land
2. Insurance
3. Postal services
4. Betting, gaming and lotteries
5. Finance
6. Education
7. Health and welfare
8. Burial and cremation
9. Trade unions and professional bodies
10. Sport, sports competitions and physical education
11. Works of art etc.
12. Fund-raising events by charities and other qualifying bodies
13. Cultural services etc.
14. Supplies of goods where input tax cannot be recovered (from 1 March 2000)
15. Investment gold (from 1 January 2000)
Notes The descriptions of the zero-rate and exempt groups are for ease of reference only and do *not* affect the interpretation of the groups (VATA 1994, s. 96(10)). Some suppliers can unilaterally elect to waive exemption of certain land and buildings (VATA 1994, Sch. 10, para. 2–4).

Partial exemption

The partial exemption rules may restrict the amount of deductible input tax (*Value Added Tax Regulations* 1995 (SI 1995/2518), Pt. XIV; Notice 706).

De minimis limit for application of partial exemption rules:

Period	Exempt input tax not exceeding
Tax years beginning after 30/11/94	• £625 per month on average; and • 50% of total input tax for prescribed accounting period
Periods beginning between 1/4/92 and 30/11/94	• £600 per month on average

Capital goods scheme

(*Value Added Tax Regulations* 1995 (SI 1995/2518), Pt. XV; Leaflet 706/2)

From 1 April 1990 the capital goods scheme affects the acquisition, etc. by a partially exempt person for use in a business of certain items as follows:

Item	Value	Adjustment period
Computers and computer equipment	£50,000 or more	5 years
Land and buildings[(1)]	£250,000 or more	10 years (5 years where interest had less than 10 years to run on acquisition)

Where the capital goods scheme applies, any initial deduction of input tax is made in the ordinary way, but must then be reviewed over the adjustment period by reference to the use of the asset concerned.

Revised rules apply to all capital goods scheme adjustments for intervals starting on or after 10 March 1999, to ensure that such adjustments compare the later use of the asset with the actual initial deduction of input VAT, after any other partial exemption adjustments.

Note

[(1)] From 3 July 1997, the capital goods scheme affects:

- civil engineering works;
- the refurbishment or fitting out of a building by the owner.

Particulars to be shown on a valid VAT invoice

(*Value Added Tax Regulations* 1995 (SI 1995/2518), Pt. III as amended)

VAT invoices generally where supplied to a person who is also in the UK

1. An identifying number
2. The time of the supply
3. The date of issue of the document
4. The name, address and registration number of the supplier
5. The name and address of the person to whom the goods or services are supplied
6. The type of supply by reference to the following categories: (a) A supply by sale (b) A supply on hire purchase or any similar transaction (c) A supply by loan (d) A supply by way of exchange (e) A supply on hire, lease or rental (f) A supply of goods made from customer's materials (g) A supply by sale on commission (h) A supply on sale or return or similar terms, or (i) Any other type of supply which the commissioners may at any time by notice specify
7. A description sufficient to identify the goods or services supplied
8. For each description, the quantity of the goods or the extent of the services, the rate of VAT and the amount payable, excluding VAT, expressed in sterling
9. The gross total amount payable, excluding VAT, expressed in sterling
10. The rate of any cash discount offered
11. Each rate of VAT chargeable and the amount of VAT chargeable, expressed in sterling, at each such rate
12. The total amount of VAT chargeable, expressed in sterling

Persons providing VAT invoices for leasing certain motor cars must state on the invoice whether the car is a qualifying vehicle. This enables the lessee to claim the correct proportion of the VAT charged by the lessor.

The requirements for invoices concerning supplies intra-EU member states are in the *Value Added Tax Regulations* 1995 (SI 1995/2518), reg. 14(2).

Retailers' invoices

If the supplier sells directly to the public, he is only required to issue a VAT invoice if the customer requests it. Furthermore, if the supply is for *£100* (before 9 April 1991 £50) or less, *including VAT,* a less-detailed VAT invoice can be issued setting out only the following:

1. The name, address and registration number of the retailer
2. The time of the supply
3. A description sufficient to identify the goods or services supplied
4. The total amount payable including VAT
5. The rate of VAT in force at the time of the supply

See Customs Notice 700 concerning the special rules for invoices for:

- petrol, derv, paraffin and heating oil;
- credit cards;
- another form of modified VAT invoice for retailers;
- cash and carry wholesalers;
- computer invoicing; and
- calculation of VAT on invoices.

Continuous supplies of services
Certain additional particulars are required to be shown on a VAT invoice for a supply of continuous services, if the supplier chooses to use the advance invoicing facility (*Value Added Tax Regulations* 1995 (SI 1995/2518), reg. 90). Similar provisions apply for advance invoicing in respect of long leases (reg. 85) and in respect of supplies of water, gas, power, heat, refrigeration and ventilation (reg. 86).

Civil penalties, surcharge and interest

See p. 63 for reckonable dates

<table>
<tr><th>Provision</th><th colspan="2">Current civil penalty etc.</th></tr>
<tr><td>• VAT evasion:
conduct involving dishonesty[1]</td><td colspan="2">Amount of VAT evaded or sought to be evaded, subject to mitigation (up to 100%).</td></tr>
<tr><td>• Incorrect certificates as to zero-rating and reduced rate certificates re fuel and power, etc.</td><td colspan="2">Customer is liable for any loss of tax with effect from 27 July 1999. VAT chargeable if certificate had been correct minus VAT actually charged.</td></tr>
<tr><td>• Misdeclaration or neglect resulting in understatements or overclaims[1][2]</td><td colspan="2">15% of the VAT which would have been lost if the inaccuracy had not been discovered.</td></tr>
<tr><td>• Repeated misdeclarations resulting in understatements or overclaims[1][3]</td><td colspan="2">15% of the VAT which would have been lost if the inaccuracy had not been discovered.</td></tr>
<tr><td rowspan="5">• Failure to notify liability for registration or change in nature of supplies by person exempted from registration[1][4]</td><td>Period of failure</td><td>Percentage of relevant VAT</td></tr>
<tr><td>9 months or less</td><td>5%</td></tr>
<tr><td>Over 9, but not over 18 months</td><td>10%</td></tr>
<tr><td>Over 18 months</td><td>15%</td></tr>
<tr><td colspan="2">(minimum penalty £50)
However, the relevant VAT is only calculated from 1 January 1996 rather than any earlier date if the liability to register followed a transfer of a business as a going concern.</td></tr>
<tr><td rowspan="9">• Default interest
(VATA 1994, s. 74)</td><td colspan="2">For assessments calculated after 16 March 1993[5] interest does not commence from more than three years prior to the assessment date. However, interest continues to be charged until the related VAT is paid.[6]</td></tr>
<tr><td>From 6/2/2000</td><td>8.5%</td></tr>
<tr><td>6/3/99–5/2/2000</td><td>7.5%</td></tr>
<tr><td>6/1/99–5/3/99</td><td>8.5%</td></tr>
<tr><td>6/7/98–5/1/99</td><td>9.5%</td></tr>
<tr><td>6/2/96–5/7/98</td><td>6.25%</td></tr>
<tr><td>6/3/95–5/2/96</td><td>7%</td></tr>
<tr><td>6/10/94–5/3/95</td><td>6.25%</td></tr>
<tr><td>6/1/94–5/10/94</td><td>5.5%</td></tr>
</table>

Provision	Current civil penalty etc.	
• Default surcharge	1st default in surcharge period	2%
	2nd	5%
	3rd	10%
	4th or later	15%
	In the case of defaults occurring after 31 March 1992 but before 1 April 1993 the maximum surcharge rate was 20%; before 1 October 1993 a surcharge liability notice could be issued after a second default and the rate was 5% for a first default in a surcharge period, 10% for a second default, 15% for a third or later default. (£30 minimum. From 1 October 1993, if the taxpayer's return is late but no VAT is due, the surcharge is nil.) Customs generally only issue a surcharge assessment at the 2% or 5% rates for an amount of at least £200. A default surcharge can arise for persons who make monthly payments on account for return periods ending after 31 May 1996.	
• Failure to comply with tribunal direction or summons	Up to £1,000	
• Unauthorised issue of VAT invoice[1]	15% (30%: pre 1 November 1995) of the 'VAT' shown or amount attributable to VAT (minimum penalty £50)	
• Breach of walking possession agreement	50% of the VAT due or amount recoverable	
• Breach of regulatory provision (Note: such a penalty cannot be imposed without a prior written warning (VATA 1994, s. 76(2))).	• Failure to preserve records: £500	
	• Submission of return or payment is late	
	Number of relevant failures in 2 years before the failure	Greater of:
	0	£5 or $^1/_6$ of 1% of VAT due
	1	£10 or $^1/_3$ of 1% of VAT due
	2 or more	£15 or $^1/_2$ of 1% of VAT due
	• Other breaches	
	Number of relevant failures in 2 years before the failure	Prescribed daily rate £
	0	5
	1	10
	2 or more	15
	Penalty: the number of days of failure (100 maximum) multiplied by above prescribed daily rate (minimum penalty £50)	

trt trt97b Mp 114—trt 180

Provision	Current civil penalty etc.	
• Failure to submit EC sales statements[8]	1st default including that to which the default notice relates	£5 per day
	2nd	£10 per day
	3rd	£15 per day
	(maximum: 100 days — minimum: £50)	
• Inaccurate EC sales statements[8]	£100 for any material inaccuracy on a statement submitted within two years of a penalty notice (itself issued after a second materially inaccurate statement)	
• Failure to notify acquisition of excise duty goods or new means of transport[1][4]	Period of failure	Percentage of relevant VAT
	3 months or less	5
	Over 3 months but not over 6 months	10
	Over 6 months	15
• Failure to comply with requirements of scheme for investment gold[1]	17.5% of the value of the transaction concerned with effect from the passing of FA 2000	

Notes

[1] Mitigation may be available.

[2] For VAT prescribed accounting periods beginning after 30 November 1993 (although Customs normally applied the rules from 16 March 1993 (Customs News Release 32/93)) a penalty may be assessed if a return understates a person's liability by an amount which is at least the lower of:

- £1m; and
- 30% of the sum of output tax and input tax, the 'gross amount of tax'.

If a misdeclaration occurs as a result of the failure to draw the attention of Customs to an understated assessment, the reference above to the 'gross amount of tax' should be changed to the 'true amount of tax'.

Previously, a serious misdeclaration was one exceeding 30% of the true amount of tax or the greater of £10,000 and 5% of the true amount of tax.

[3] Repeated misdeclaration penalty may be assessed if:

- there are three or more misdeclared returns within 12 accounting periods;
- the misdeclaration in each period equals or exceeds the lesser of 10% of the 'gross amount of tax' (see [2]) and £500,000;
- Customs have issued a penalty liability notice; and
- at least two further misdeclarations occur during the eight periods completed following the issue of a penalty liability notice. This includes the period in which the notice is issued.

The above conditions apply to VAT prescribed accounting periods beginning after 30 November 1993, although Customs normally applied the rules from 16 March 1993 (Customs News Release 32/93).

[4] The rates given relate to original assessments made on or after 1 January 1995.

[5] Officially the capping of interest applies to interest on any assessment calculated on or after 1 October 1993, however Customs normally applied the new rules from 16 March 1993 when they were announced (Customs News Release 32/93).

[6] Customs generally do not charge interest where it does not represent commercial restitution (News Release 34/94, 7 September 1994).

[7] Intrastats (supplementary statistical declarations) – criminal offences:

- failure to submit declaration or to provide requested information – fine up to £2,500 (level 4 on the standard scale);
- a trader who knowingly or recklessly makes a false return, or falsifies a return, is:
  (a) on summary conviction, liable to a fine up to £2,500 (level 4 on the standard scale) and/or three months imprisonment; and
  (b) on indictment, liable to an unlimited fine and/or imprisonment up to two years.

[8] With effect from 27 July 1999 there is a two-year time-limit for assessing penalties relating to EC sales statements.

Flat-rate scheme for farmers

(VATA 1994, s. 54)

Period of application	Flat-rate addition %
From 1/1/93	4

Interest on overpaid VAT

Interest on overpaid VAT arises under VATA 1994, s. 78 in certain cases of official error:

Period of application	Rate %
From 6 February 2000	5
6 March 1999 to 5 February 2000	4
6 January 1999 to 5 March 1999	5
1 April 1997 to 5 January 1999	6
6 February 1993 to 31 March 1997	8

Note

Generally, a repayment under VATA 1994, s. 78 in relation to any claim made after 18 July 1996 is not made for more than three years after the end of the applicable period to which it relates.

'Blocked' input tax

Any input tax charged on the following items is 'blocked', i.e. non-recoverable:

- motor cars, other than certain motor cars acquired by certain persons but after 31 July 1995 (1) any person can recover input tax on motor cars used exclusively for business and (2) only 50 per cent of VAT on car leasing charges is recoverable if lessee makes any private use of the car and if lessor recovered the VAT on buying the car;
- entertainment, except of employees;
- in the case of claims by builders, articles of a kind not ordinarily installed by builders as fixtures in new houses;
- goods supplied under the second-hand scheme;
- goods imported for private purposes;
- non-business element of supplies to be used only partly for business purposes. This may contravene European law where the supplies are of goods: strictly the input tax is deductible, but output tax is due on non-business use. VAT on supplies not intended for business use does not rank as input tax, so cannot be recovered;
- goods and services acquired by a tour operator for re-supply as a designated travel service; and
- domestic accommodation for directors and their families to the extent of domestic purpose use.

In addition, 'exempt input tax' is not recoverable. From 10 March 1999, the partial exemption simplification rule that allowed some businesses to claim back all their input tax, providing that their exempt input tax is only incurred in relation to certain exempt supplies has been abolished.

VAT on private fuel

(VATA 1994, s. 56)

For prescribed accounting periods *beginning* after 5 April 2000, the following table applies to assess output tax due on fuel used by cars for private journeys if it was provided at below cost from business resources. There is no high business mileage discount.

	12 months £	VAT due per car £	3 months £	VAT due per car £	1 month £	VAT due per car £
Diesel						
Cylinder capacity: 2,000cc or less	930	138.51	232	34.55	77	11.46
over 2,000cc	1,180	175.74	295	43.93	98	14.59
Petrol						
Cylinder capacity: 1,400cc or less	1,025	152.65	256	38.12	85	12.65
over 1,400cc up to 2,000cc	1,300	193.61	325	48.40	108	16.08
over 2,000cc	1,915	285.21	478	71.19	159	23.68

For prescribed accounting periods *beginning* before 6 April 2000 but after 5 April 1998, the following table applies to assess output tax due on fuel used by cars for private journeys if it was provided at below cost from business resources. There is no high business mileage discount.

	12 months £	VAT due per car £	3 months £	VAT due per car £	1 month £	VAT due per car £
Diesel						
Cylinder capacity: 2,000cc or less	785	116.91	196	29.19	65	9.68
over 2,000cc	995	148.19	248	36.93	82	12.21
Petrol						
Cylinder capacity: 1,400cc or less	850	126.59	212	31.57	70	10.42
over 1,400cc up to 2,000cc	1,075	160.10	268	39.91	89	13.25
over 2,000cc	1,585	236.00	396	58.97	132	19.65

VAT publications having legal force

The VAT publications that have legal force are listed in Notice 747.

trt trt97b Mp 117—trt 180

INSURANCE PREMIUM TAX

Rate

Imposed on certain insurance premiums where the risk is located in the UK.

Period of application	Standard rate %	Higher rate %
From 1 July 1999	5	17.5
1 April 1997 to 30 June 1999	4	17.5
1 October 1994 to 31 March 1997	2.5	n/a

Note
From 1 August 1998, the higher rate applies to all travel insurance.

Interest payable on certain assessments

Period of application	Rate %
From 6 February 2000	8.5
6 March 1999 to 5 February 2000	7.5
6 January 1999 to 5 March 1999	8.5
6 July 1998 to 5 January 1999	9.5
6 February 1996 to 5 July 1998	6.25
1 October 1994 to 5 February 1996	5.5

LANDFILL TAX

Landfill tax was introduced on 1 October 1996 and is collected from landfill site operators.

Exemption applies to mining and quarrying waste, dredging waste, pet cemeteries and waste from the reclamation of contaminated land.

From 1 October 1999 exemption applies to inert waste used in restoring licensed landfill sites, including the progressive backfilling of active mineral workings.

Type of waste	Rate (per tonne) £
Inactive waste	2
Active waste:	
1 April 2004 to 31 March 2005	15
1 April 2003 to 31 March 2004	14
1 April 2002 to 31 March 2003	13
1 April 2001 to 31 March 2002	12
1 April 2000 to 31 March 2001	11
1 April 1999 to 31 March 2000	10
1 October 1996 to 31 March 1999	7

Environmental trusts

Site operators making payments to environmental trusts set up for approved environmental purposes can claim a tax credit up to 90 per cent of their contribution – subject to a maximum of 20 per cent of their landfill tax bill in a 12-month period. From 1 August 1999 operators using the scheme will have up to an additional month every quarter to claim tax credits. On 15 October 1996, Customs approved an independent body, ENTRUST, as the regulator of environmental trusts. It is responsible for enrolling environmental bodies, maintaining their operation and ensuring that all expenditure complies with the landfill tax regulations.

trt trt97b Mp 119—trt 180

INDEX

References are to page numbers

Page

A

AA estimated standing and running costs 20; 21

Accumulation and discretionary trusts
. income tax rates 5

Additional allowance for children 2

Advance corporation tax
. abolition 46
. due dates 47
. elections and claims, time-limits 50–53
. interest 64
. rates 46

Age allowance 2

Agricultural and forestry land and buildings allowances 55

Agricultural property relief 95

Aircraft
. roll-over relief 90

Annual exemption
. capital gains tax 80
. inheritance tax 96

Arrears of tax
. official error 69

Artificial transactions in land
. clearance procedures 76

Attendance allowance 35; 36

B

Back to work bonus 35

Basis of assessment
. elections and claims 31

Beneficial loans
. foreign currency loans 30
. official rate of interest 30

Benefits in kind
. beneficial loans 30
. company vehicles and fuel – see Cars and vans
. returns 9

Blind person's allowance 2

Business expansion scheme 27

Business property relief 95

Page

C

Capital allowances
. agricultural and forestry land and buildings 55
. cars 55
. claims, time-limits 52
. claims under self-assessment, time-limits 53
. dredging 56
. dwelling-houses let on assured tenancies 56
. enterprise zones 56
. hotels 55
. industrial buildings allowances 55
. know-how 56
. lease rentals for expensive cars 59
. long-life assets 55
. machinery and plant
. . rates 55
. . short-life assets 32
. mineral extraction 56
. mines and oil wells etc. 56
. patent rights 56
. rates 56; 57
. scientific research 56
. set-off, time-limits 52
. ships 55
. transfers between connected persons, time-limits 32; 52

Capital gains tax
. annual exempt amount 80
. charities 91
. chattel exemption 80
. claims, time-limits 92
. due dates 80
. elections, time-limits 9
. enterprise investment scheme 89
. indexation allowance 81–87
. interest 63
. leases which are wasting assets 81
. personal representatives' expenses 91
. rates and thresholds 80
. retail prices index 71
. retirement relief 90
. roll-over relief, classes of assets 90
. surcharges 63
. taper relief 88
. venture capital trusts 28
. wasting assets 81

Capital goods scheme 111

Page

Capital transfer tax – see Inheritance tax

Cars and vans
. AA estimated standing and running costs 20; 21
. benefit scales 16; 17
. capital allowances 55
. . lease rentals for expensive cars 59
. fuel benefit scales 18; 19
. mileage allowances, fixed profit car scheme 22
. mobile telephones 19
. National Insurance contributions 43
. value added tax, private fuel 117
. van benefit scales 19

Cash donations
. gift aid 59

Certificates of tax deposit
. Series 7 .... 61; 62

Charities
. capital gains tax 91
. gift aid 59
. payroll giving scheme 25

Chattel exemption 80

Child benefit 35; 36

Childcare tax credits 3; 4

Children
. additional allowance for 2
. child benefit 35; 36
. maintenance bonus 35
. settlements on 26
. small maintenance payments 25

Christmas bonus 35; 36

Claims
. advance corporation tax, carry-back/ surrender 50
. capital gains tax, time-limits 92
. corporation tax, time-limits 50–53
. group relief 51
. income tax, time-limits 31
. losses 32

Clearance procedures 76; 77

Clearing systems 79

Close companies
. gift aid 59
. loans to participators 46; 47; 49

Close investment-holding companies (CICs)
. corporation tax 45

Page

Clothing allowances
. flat rate allowances 22
. uniform allowances 22

Company reconstructions and amalgamations
. clearance procedures 77

Company vehicles and fuel – see Cars and vans

Conveyance or transfer on sale
. stamp duty 100

Corporation tax
. advance corporation tax rates 46
. claims, time-limits 50–53
. due dates 47
. elections, time-limits 50–53
. filing deadlines 48
. instalment payments 47
. interest 49; 64; 67
. marginal relief 46
. pay and file 47; 49
. penalties 49
. rates 45
. repayment interest 50; 67
. repayment supplement 66
. self-assessment 47
. . overpaid 68
. . unpaid 67
. small companies' rate 45
. unpaid/late paid, interest 67

Council tax benefit 35

Criminal injuries compensation 35

Cycles
. authorised rate 22

D

Dates for payment of tax
. capital gains tax 80
. corporation tax 47
. income tax 10
. inheritance tax 94
. pay and file 47

Death
. capital gains tax claims 92
. inheritance tax – see Inheritance tax
. personal representatives' expenses 91

Default interest – see Interest rates

Delivery of accounts
. inheritance tax 97

Demergers
. clearance procedures 76

Page

Dependent adults' benefits 34

De-registration limits
. value added tax 107

Disabled persons
. constant attendance allowance 35
. disability living allowance 35; 36
. severe disablement allowance 35; 36
. tax credit 4

Disease scheme benefits 35

Distributions 45

Dividend income 45

Double tax treaties 75

Dredging allowances 56

Dwelling-houses let on assured tenancies
. capital allowances 56

E

Education welfare benefits 35

Elections
. advance corporation tax, carry-back/ surrender 50
. capital gains tax, time-limits 92
. corporation tax, time-limits 50–53
. income tax, time-limits 31

Employee share ownership trusts (ESOPs/ESOTs)
. clearance procedures 77

Employee share schemes
. all-employee share plans 14
. clearance procedures 76
. company share option plans 15
. profit sharing schemes – see Profit sharing schemes
. savings-related – see Savings-related share option schemes

Employment rehabilitation allowance 35

Enterprise investment scheme
. capital gains tax 89
. income tax 27

Enterprise management incentives 16

Enterprise zones
. capital allowances 56
. designated 57

Entertainers and sportsmen
. non-residents, clearance procedures for withholding tax 77
. retirement ages 13

Page

Exemptions
. capital gains tax 80
. inheritance tax 96
. value added tax 110

Ex gratia payments 14

Expenses
. incidental overnight expenses 24
. personal representatives 91

F

Family allowance – see Child benefit

Farming and market gardening
. elections and claims, time-limits 31
. fluctuating profits 10
. quotas, roll-over relief 90
. value added tax flat rate scheme 115

Fish quotas
. roll-over relief 90

Fixed profit car scheme – see Cars and vans

Flat rate allowances 22

Foreign currency loans
. official rate of interest 30

Foreign earnings deduction 23

Foreign exchange gains and losses
. loss relief, time-limits 52
. rates 72–74

Foreign income 23

Forestry land and buildings allowance 55

Forms
. PAYE returns 9

FOTRA securities 29

Fuel scale charges – see Cars and vans

Furnished lettings 2; 3

Futures exchanges 78

G

Gift aid 59

Gifts
. assets 60
. charities 25; 59
. hold-over gain, time-limits 92
. inheritance tax 96

Gilt-edged securities
. non-residents holding 29

Page

Goodwill
. roll-over relief 90

Groups of companies
. group relief, time-limits for elections and claims 51
. surrender of company tax refund, time-limits 51

Guardian's allowance 35; 36

H

Hold-over relief
. time-limits for elections and claims 92

Hospital down rating 34

Hotels
. capital allowances 54

Housing benefit 35

Hovercraft
. roll-over relief 90

Husband and wife
. additional allowance for children 2
. age allowance 2
. married couple's allowance 2; 31

I

Incapacity benefit 34; 35, 36

Incidental overnight expenses 24

Income support 35; 37; 38

Income tax
. beneficial loans, official rate of interest 30
. business expansion scheme 27
. claims, time-limits 31
. company vehicles and fuel – see Cars and vans
. due dates 10
. elections, time-limits 31
. enterprise investment scheme 27
. farming and market gardening, fluctuating profits 10
. flat rate allowance 22
. foreign employees' liability 23
. gilt-edged securities 29
. income arising outside UK 23
. individual savings accounts 26
. interest 63
. National Savings Bank interest 33
. PAYE – see PAYE
. payments on loss of office or employment 14

Page

. payroll giving scheme 25
. penalty provisions 6; 9
. personal equity plans (PEPs) 26
. personal pension schemes – see Personal pension schemes
. personal reliefs 2
. personal tax returns, filing date 6
. profit-related pay schemes 16
. profit sharing schemes 14
. rates 5
. relocation allowance 24
. retirement annuities – see Retirement annuities
. settlements on children 26
. small maintenance payments 25
. state benefits
. . non-taxable 35; 36
. . taxable 34
. statutory maternity pay 35
. statutory sick pay 33
. surcharges 63
. tax-exempt special savings accounts (TESSAs) 25
. termination payments 14
. venture capital trusts 28

Indexation allowance 81–87

Individual savings accounts (ISAs) 26

Industrial buildings allowance 55

Industrial death benefit 34

Industrial injuries disablement benefit 35

Information technology equipment
. capital allowances 55

Inheritance tax
. agricultural property relief 95
. business property relief 95
. delivery of accounts 97
. due dates 94
. excepted estates 99
. exemptions 96
. gifts
. . annual and small 96
. . in consideration of marriage 96
. instalment payments 96
. lifetime transfers
. . delivery of accounts 97
. . due dates for payment 94
. . rates of tax 93
. penalties 98
. prescribed rates of interest 94
. quick succession relief 96
. reliefs 95
. taper relief 94

Page

. transfers on death
. . delivery of accounts 97
. . due dates for payment 94
. . rates of tax 93
. values below which no account required 99

Insurance premium tax 118

Interest
. advance corporation tax 64
. capital gains tax 63
. corporation tax 64
. income tax 63
. National Insurance contributions 44; 64
. rates – see Interest rates
. termination of savings-related share option scheme 15

Interest rates
. beneficial loans 30
. . foreign currency loans 30
. certificates of tax deposit 61; 62
. corporation tax 67–69
. inheritance tax 94
. investigation settlements 66
. official rate 30
. overdue tax 65
. . interest factor tables 65
. . official error 69
. . recovery of tax to make good loss due to taxpayer's fault 66
. overpaid tax, repayment supplement 66
. PAYE 10; 64
. prescribed rates
. . inheritance tax 94
. . value added tax 64; 113–115
. repaymentinterest 67–69
. repayment supplement 66
. stamp duty 101
. stamp duty reserve tax 102
. value added tax
. . default interest 113–115
. . overpaid 116
. . prescribed 64; 113–115

Invalid care allowance 34

Investment exchanges 79

Investment income
. election for split 31

Investment trusts
. personal equity plans (PEPs), limit on holding 25

Invoices
. value added tax 112

Page

J

Jobseeker's allowance 37; 38

K

Know-how 56

L

Land and buildings
. roll-over relief 90

Landfill tax 119

Lease premiums
. chargeable gains 58
. Schedule A 58
. stamp duty 101

Leases
. stamp duty 101
. wasting assets 81

Letters of allotment
. stamp duty 100

Life assurance premium relief 2

Lifetime transfers – see Inheritance tax

Loans – see also Beneficial loans
. interest rates – see Interest rates
. irrecoverable loans to traders, claims 92

Lone parent's benefit 35

Losses – see Trading losses

M

Machinery and plant allowances
. disclaimer of writing-down allowances, time-limits 52
. fixed, roll-over relief 90
. gift aid 60
. notification of expenditure, time-limits 52
. rates 55
. short life assets, claims 32; 51

Main residence
. determination, time-limits 92

Maintenance funds for historic buildings
. clearance procedures 76

Maintenance payments
. small 25

Married couple's allowance
. election to transfer 31
. rate 2

Page

Maternity allowance 35; 36

Medical expenses
. incurred in the EEA 35

Mileage allowances – see Cars and vans

Millennium gift aid 59

Mineral extraction
. capital allowances 56

Mines and oil wells
. capital allowances 56

Mobile telephones 19

Mortgage interest relief
. allocation 31
. loan limit 2

Motability 35

Motor cycles
. authorised rate 22

N

National Insurance contributions
. Class 1 39–42
. . late payments, interest 44
. . return deadlines 43
. Class 1A 43
. . late payments, interest 44
. . return deadlines 43
. Class 1B 43
. Class 2 43
. Class 3 44
. Class 4 44
. company vehicles and fuel 43
. . interest 44
. . return deadlines 43
. interest on unpaid 44
. return deadlines for Class 1 and 1A 43

National Savings Bank interest 33

Non-residents
. entertainers and sportsmen, clearance procedures for withholding tax 77
. gilt-edged securities 29
. liability to UK tax 23

Northern Ireland
. capital allowances 55

O

Offences – see Penalties

Offshore funds
. clearance procedures 76

Page

Overdue tax
. interest rates – see Interest rates

Overpaid tax
. repayment supplement 66

Overseas income 23

P

Partnerships
. elections and claims, time-limits 31
. penalty provisions 7
. retirement annuities, earned income limit 12

Patent rights 56

Pay and file
. due dates 47
. filing deadlines 48
. repayment interest 67

PAYE
. code numbers 8
. interest on late payments 10
. interest on overdue tax 64
. penalties 9
. return deadlines 9
. settlement agreements, Class 1B National Insurance contributions 43
. thresholds 8

Payments on account
. interim payments 10

Payroll giving scheme 25

P11D and P9D returns 9

Penalties – see also Interest rates
. chargeability, failure to notify 6
. false statements 6
. incorrect returns 6; 10
. individuals 6
. inheritance tax 98
. investigations, failure to produce documents 6
. late returns 6
. partnerships 7
. PAYE 9
. records, failure to keep 6
. stamp duties 102; 103
. standard scale 70
. value added tax 113–115

Personal allowance 2

Personal equity plans (PEPs) 26

Personal pension schemes
. contributions
. . carry-back, time-limits 32

Page

. . earnings cap ... 11
. . limit of allowable payment ... 11
. early retirement ages ... 12; 13

Personal reliefs ... 2

Personal representatives
. expenses ... 91
. taper relief ... 88

Petrol – see Cars and vans

Plant and machinery – see Machinery and plant allowances

Post-cessation expenses
. claims for relief, time-limits ... 31; 92

Premiums for leases – see Lease premiums

Prescribed rates of interest – see Interest rates

Profit-related pay schemes
. limit on tax-free amount ... 16

Profit sharing schemes
. clearance procedures ... 76
. maximum value of shares ... 15

Purchase by company of own shares
. clearance procedures ... 76
. stamp duty ... 100

Q

Quick succession relief ... 96

Quotas
. roll-over relief ... 90

R

Re-basing of assets
. time-limits for claims ... 92

Recognised clearing systems ... 79

Recognised futures exchanges ... 78

Recognised investment exchanges ... 79

Recognised stock exchanges ... 77

Reconstructions and amalgamations
. clearance procedures ... 77

Reduced earnings allowance ... 35

Registration limits
. value added tax ... 106

Relocation allowances
. statutory and concessionary relief ... 24

Page

Remission of tax
. official error ... 69

Rent-a-room limit ... 2

Repayment interest
. corporation tax ... 50; 67
. pay and file ... 67

Repayment supplement
. factor tables ... 66

Replacement of business assets – see Roll-over relief

Residence – see Main residence

Retail prices index ... 71

Retirement ages ... 12; 13; 34

Retirement annuities
. early retirement ages ... 12; 13
. partners, earned income limit ... 12
. premiums
. . carry-back, time-limits ... 32
. . limit of allowable payment ... 11

Retirement pension ... 34

Retirement relief
. annual thresholds ... 90
. time-limits for claims ... 92

Returns
. corporation tax, filing deadlines ... 48
. National Insurance contributions, Class 1 and 1A ... 43
. partnerships, penalty provisions ... 7
. pay and file ... 48
. PAYE deadlines ... 9
. penalties ... 6; 9; 49
. personal tax returns, filing date ... 6

Roll-over relief
. classes of assets ... 90
. time-limits ... 92

S

Satellites, space stations and spacecraft
. roll-over relief ... 90

Savings income
. income tax rate ... 5
. individual savings accounts ... 26
. National Savings Bank interest ... 33
. personal equity plans ... 26
. tax-exempt special savings accounts ... 26

Savings-related share option schemes
. bonus and interest payments on termination ... 15

Savings-related share option schemes – continued — Page
. clearance procedures 76
. monthly contributions 15

Scientific research allowances 56

Settlement agreements
. PAYE, Class 1B National Insurance contributions 43

Settlements on children 26

Severe disablement allowance 35

Share schemes
. all-employee share plans 14
. company plans, maximum value of shares under option 15
. savings-related – see Savings-related share option schemes

Shares, debentures and securities
. acquisition on or after 6 April 1998 89
. clearance procedures 76
. stamp duty – see Stamp duties

Ships
. capital allowances 55
. roll-over relief 90

Small companies' rate 45

Small maintenance payments 25

Social fund payments 35

Sportsmen – see Entertainers and sportsmen

Stamp duties
. abolitions since March 1985 105
. fixed duties 101
. interest rates 101
. penalties 102; 103
. prospective abolitions 105
. rates
. . conveyance or transfer on sale 100
. . leases 101
. stamp duty reserve tax 102
. . interest 102

State benefits
. not taxable 35; 36
. taxable 34

Statutory maternity pay (SMP) 35

Statutory redundancy payments 35

Statutory sick pay (SSP) 33

Stock exchanges 77

Stock transfer
. stamp duty 100

Sci

Page

T

Take overs and mergers
. stamp duty 100

Taper relief
. capital gains tax 88
. enterprise investment scheme 27
. inheritance tax 94

Tax credits
. abolition 45

Tax-exempt special savings accounts (TESSAs) 26

Telephones
. mobile telephones 19

Terminal losses
. carry-back, time-limits 32

Termination payments 14

TESSAs 26

Time-limits
. corporation tax, filing deadlines 48
. elections and claims
. . capital gains tax 92
. . corporation tax 50–53
. . income tax 31

Tools and special clothing allowances 22

Trading losses
. elections and claims
. . capital gains tax 92
. . corporation tax 50
. . income tax 32

Trading stock
. millennium gift aid 59
. valuation, transfer on cessation of trade 31; 50

Transactions in securities
. clearance procedures 76

Transfer of trades between member states
. clearance procedures 77

Transfers on death – see Inheritance tax

Trustees
. capital gains tax rate 80
. taper relief 88

U

Uniform allowances 22

Unquoted shares in trading companies
. set-off of loss, time-limits 32; 51

Page

V

Vaccine damage 35

Valuation of assets
. capital gains tax, time-limits 92

Value added tax
. capital goods scheme 111
. cash accounting 108
. civil penalties 113–115
. default interest and default surcharge 64; 113–115
. de-registration limits 107
. exempt supplies 110
. flat-rate scheme for farmers 115
. input tax blocked 116
. interest rates 64; 113–116
. invoices 112
. misdeclaration penalty 113–115
. partial exemption 110
. private fuel 117
. publications having legal force 117
. rates 106
. registration limits 106
. repeated misdeclaration penalty 113–115
. zero-rated supplies 109

Vans – see Cars and vans

Page

Venture capital trusts (VCTs) 28

W

War disablement pension 35

War pensioner's mobility supplement 35

War widow's pension 35

Wasting assets
. leases 81

Widowed mother's allowance 34; 35

Widow's benefit 34

Widow's bereavement allowance 2

Widow's payment 34; 35

Worker's compensation scheme 35

Working abroad 23

Working families tax credit (WFTC) 3

Z

Zero-rated supplies
. value added tax 109